I0448197

March 2013

MAJOR AUTOMATED INFORMATION SYSTEMS

Selected Defense Programs Need to Implement Key Acquisition Practices

GAO

Accountability ★ Integrity ★ Reliability

GAO Highlights

Highlights of GAO-13-311, a report to congressional addressees

MAJOR AUTOMATED INFORMATION SYSTEMS

Selected Defense Programs Need to Implement Key Acquisition Practices

Why GAO Did This Study

In 2011, DOD allotted at least $5.6 billion for designated MAIS programs, which are intended to help the department sustain its key operations. The National Defense Authorization Act for Fiscal Year 2012 mandated that GAO select and assess DOD MAIS programs annually through March 2018. This report discusses the results of GAO's first annual assessment. The act directed GAO to (1) describe the extent to which selected MAIS programs have stayed within planned cost and schedule estimates and met performance targets, (2) assess selected MAIS programs' actions to manage risks, and (3) assess the extent to which selected MAIS programs used key information technology acquisition best practices.

To do so, GAO selected 14 of the 48 DOD MAIS programs based on several factors, including size of total life-cycle costs, and summarized the results of analyses of cost, schedule, and performance across the programs. Further, GAO selected 3 of the 14 programs (one Army, one Air Force, and one Navy) and analyzed their risk management actions and assessed them against best practices for requirements management and project monitoring and control.

What GAO Recommends

GAO recommends that DOD direct the Army program to address weaknesses in its risk management and IV&V practices. DOD concurred with these two recommendations and provided additional information that removed the need for a third potential recommendation regarding leadership on the Air Force program.

View GAO-13-311. For more information, contact Valerie C. Melvin at (202) 512-6304 or melvinv@gao.gov.

What GAO Found

Of the 14 selected Department of Defense (DOD) major automated information system (MAIS) programs, 9 had stayed within their planned cost estimates, while 5 did not (with cost increases ranging from 3 to 578 percent); 5 programs remained on schedule, while 9 experienced delays (ranging from 6 months to 10 years); and 8 programs met their system performance targets, while 5 did not fully meet their targets, and 1 did not have system performance data available. Looking at these areas collectively, 3 programs stayed within their planned cost and schedule estimates and met their system performance targets, and 2 programs experienced shortcomings in all of the areas—cost, schedule, and performance.

The three selected programs demonstrated mixed results in effectively defining and managing risks of various levels. Specifically, Navy's Consolidated Afloat Networks and Enterprise Services had implemented key practices for risk management, including identifying risks that could negatively affect work efforts. In contrast, the Air Force's Defense Enterprise Accounting and Management System's risk reports were out of date and not regularly updated to include the current status of mitigation actions. To its credit, the program had recently taken steps to improve its risk management process, such as establishing a risk and issues working group. These recent steps should help the program effectively identify and manage program risks going forward. Finally, Global Combat Support System-Army had developed program risks and mitigation plans, but the program was using multiple risk management systems that contained inconsistent data. Until the program establishes a risk management system that includes a comprehensive and up-to-date log of all current threats to the program, it will lack assurance that it is appropriately mitigating all identified risks.

The three selected programs demonstrated mixed progress in implementing key requirements management and project monitoring and control best practices. Specifically, the Navy and Army programs had implemented key requirements management best practices. However, while the Air Force program had also implemented selected practices, it had not traced all of its lower-level requirements to its desired higher-level system capabilities—which is inconsistent with requirements management best practices. Program officials stated that they expect this mapping to be completed by the fourth quarter of fiscal year 2013. Regarding project monitoring and control practices, the Navy program had implemented key best practices, while the Air Force and Army programs lacked certain practices. For example, while the Air Force program regularly communicated with its stakeholders, it had not ensured stable leadership—having four program managers in the past 4 years. DOD commented that it supports tenure agreements, with the first two program managers each completing 3-year terms. While the third and fourth program managers did not complete 3-year tenures, DOD stated that it expects the current program manager to do so. Further, while the Army program also met with stakeholders, it did not effectively use its independent verification and validation (IV&V) function to monitor its program. Until the Army program specifies the roles and responsibilities of the IV&V agent to ensure that it maintains its independence from the risk management processes that it reviews, the program jeopardizes its ability to fully monitor and control the program.

_____ United States Government Accountability Office

Contents

Figures

Abbreviations

APB	acquisition program baseline
CAC2S	Common Aviation Command and Control System
CANES	Consolidated Afloat Networks and Enterprise Services
CMMI-ACQ	Capability Maturity Model® Integration for Acquisition
DCGS-N	Distributed Common Ground System-Navy
DEAMS	Defense Enterprise Accounting and Management System
DOD	Department of Defense
ECSS	Expeditionary Combat Support System
FIRST	Financial Information Resource System
GCCS-A	Global Command and Control System-Army
GCSS-Army	Global Combat Support System-Army
GCSS-J	Global Combat Support System-Joint
IT	information technology
ITS	Information Transport Services
IV&V	independent verification and validation
MAIS	major automated information system
MPS	Mission Planning Systems
Navy ERP	Navy Enterprise Resource Planning
TMC	Tactical Mission Command

This is a work of the U.S. government and is not subject to copyright protection in the United States. The published product may be reproduced and distributed in its entirety without further permission from GAO. However, because this work may contain copyrighted images or other material, permission from the copyright holder may be necessary if you wish to reproduce this material separately.

G A O
Accountability * Integrity * Reliability

United States Government Accountability Office
Washington, DC 20548

March 28, 2013

Congressional Addressees

The Department of Defense (DOD) is one of the largest and most complex organizations in the world. To meet its mission, it relies heavily on the use of information technology (IT). In this regard, according to DOD's IT investment portfolio for fiscal year 2011, the department allotted approximately $36.6 billion for its IT investments.[1] Of this amount, at least $5.6 billion was allotted for major automated information system (MAIS) programs, which are intended to help the department sustain its key operations.[2]

DOD IT investments that fall within one of the following categories are designated as MAIS programs: (1) program costs in any single year exceed $32 million, (2) total program acquisition costs exceed $126 million, or (3) total life-cycle costs exceed $378 million.[3] The Secretary of Defense can also use discretion to designate a program as a MAIS if it does not meet these cost thresholds.

The National Defense Authorization Act for Fiscal Year 2012 mandated that GAO select and assess DOD MAIS programs annually through March 2018.[4] Our objectives for this first assessment were to (1) describe the extent to which selected MAIS programs have stayed within planned cost and schedule estimates and met performance targets, (2) assess selected MAIS programs' actions to manage risks, and (3) assess the extent to which selected MAIS programs have used key IT acquisition best practices.

---

[1]DOD's IT investment portfolio identifies all of its IT investments and associated costs within the department and its components.

[2]The $5.6 billion represents the amount that DOD allotted in fiscal year 2011 for 42 of 48 2011 MAIS programs. Budget information was not available for the remaining 6 programs.

[3]10 U.S.C. § 2445a(a).

[4]Pub. L. No. 112-81, § 1078 (2011) requires that we report on these assessments no later than March 30 of each year from 2013 through 2018. In November 2011, prior to the enactment of this law, the Chairman and former Ranking Member of the Senate Armed Services committee requested that we begin an assessment of DOD MAIS programs.

To accomplish the first objective, we selected 14 of the 48 MAIS programs listed in DOD's 2011 MAIS annual reports for evaluation, since these were the most recent reports available at the time we started this review.[5] To select these programs, we first identified programs that met several criteria, including those that had an acquisition program baseline (APB),[6] were not using firm fixed-price contracts for the majority of development work, had the largest planned total life-cycle costs, and represented multiple DOD components. This analysis resulted in a selection of 10 programs. Next, we selected two additional programs that had the largest planned total life-cycle costs and met all of the above selection criteria except they were using firm fixed-price contracts. The final two programs were selected based on the fact that they had been without APBs for the longest periods of time.

To determine the extent to which each of the 14 programs had stayed within their planned cost and schedule estimates, we compared the cost and schedule estimates established in the first APB to the latest planned total life-cycle cost estimates (in then-year dollars) and schedule estimates.[7] In order to determine whether the programs experienced significant or critical deviations in their cost and schedule estimates, we compared any deviations to thresholds established by statute.[8] Specifically, according to the statute, a program is considered to have undergone a "significant" change when it has (1) experienced a schedule

---

[5]The 14 MAIS programs included in our review were: Air Force's Defense Enterprise Accounting and Management System (DEAMS) Increment 1, Expeditionary Combat Support System (ECSS) Increment 1, Financial Information Resource System (FIRST), Information Transport Services (ITS) Increment 1, and Mission Planning Systems (MPS) Increment 4; Army's Global Combat Support System – Army (GCSS-Army); Global Command and Control System – Army (GCCS-A) Block 4; and Tactical Mission Command (TMC); Defense Information Systems Agency's (DISA) Global Combat Support System – Joint (GCSS-J) Increment 7 and Teleport Generation 3; and Navy's Common Aviation Command and Control System (CAC2S) Increment 1, Consolidated Afloat Networks and Enterprise Services (CANES), Distributed Common Ground System – Navy (DCGS-N) Increment 1, and Navy Enterprise Resource Planning (Navy ERP).

[6]A program's APB contains the life-cycle cost estimate, schedule estimate, and performance parameters that were approved for that program by the milestone decision authority. The first APB is established after the program has assessed the viability of various technologies and refined user requirements to identify the most appropriate technology solution that demonstrates that it can meet users' needs.

[7]An estimate in then-year dollars includes the effects of economic inflation.

[8]10 U.S.C. § 2445c.

change that will cause a delay of more than 6 months but less than a year; (2) experienced an estimated development or full life-cycle cost increase of at least 15 percent, but less than 25 percent, over the original estimate; or (3) experienced a significant, adverse change in the expected performance of the system. A program is considered to have undergone a "critical" change" when it has (1) experienced a schedule change that will cause a delay of 1 year or more; (2) experienced an estimated development or full life-cycle cost increase of 25 percent or more over the original estimate; (3) failed to achieve a full deployment decision within 5 years after the milestone A decision for the program or, if there was no milestone A decision, the date when the preferred alternative was selected for the program; or (4) experienced a change in the expected performance of the system or major IT investment to be acquired under the program that will undermine the ability of the system to perform the functions anticipated.[9]

Additionally, to determine whether system performance targets were met, we analyzed each program's system performance targets against actual performance data, and reviewed the results of operational assessments and program evaluations conducted on the systems. We then aggregated and summarized the results of our cost, schedule, and performance analyses across the 14 programs, as well as developed individual program profiles, which are presented in appendix II.

To address the second objective, we selected 3 of the 14 programs from the first objective based on two criteria, including two programs that had the highest planned total life-cycle costs and one program that had been without a baseline for the longest period of time.[10] To assess each program's actions to manage risks, we identified key risk management practices from the Software Engineering Institute's Capability Maturity Model® Integration for Acquisition (CMMI-ACQ), and assessed each of the three programs against these criteria. Specifically, for each of the three selected programs, we analyzed risk management documentation, such as risk logs and mitigation plans, to identify levels of risks and determine the status of each program's key risks and the actions that were taken to manage these risks. Additionally, we interviewed program officials about the risks and risk management practices that they used.

---

[9]A milestone A decision authorizes acquisition of the program.

[10]The three selected MAIS programs are CANES, DEAMS, and GCSS-Army.

GAO-13-311 Defense Major Automated Information Systems

To address the third objective, we selected the same three programs as in objective two to determine the extent to which each program was implementing (1) requirements management and (2) project monitoring and control best practices, as defined by CMMI-ACQ. We also assessed these programs against key best practices for employing independent verification and validation (IV&V).[11] To determine the extent to which each program's acquisition practices were consistent with these best practices, we assessed program management and systems documentation, such as program requirements and program management reports. We also interviewed program officials to obtain additional information on each program's IT management processes in these areas.

We conducted this performance audit from January 2012 to March 2013 in accordance with generally accepted government auditing standards. Those standards require that we plan and perform the audit to obtain sufficient, appropriate evidence to provide a reasonable basis for our findings and conclusions based on our audit objectives. We believe that the evidence obtained provides a reasonable basis for our findings and conclusions based on our audit objectives. See appendix I for a more detailed discussion of our objectives, scope, and methodology.

Background

DOD is a massive and complex organization. It includes the Office of the Secretary of Defense, the Joint Chiefs of Staff, the military departments, numerous defense agencies and field activities, and various unified combatant commands that contribute to the oversight of DOD's acquisition programs. Figure 1 presents a simplified depiction of DOD's organizational structure.

---

[11]GAO, *Information Technology: DHS Needs to Improve Its Independent Acquisition Reviews*, GAO-11-581 (Washington, D.C.: July 28, 2011).

Figure 1: Simplified DOD Organizational Structure

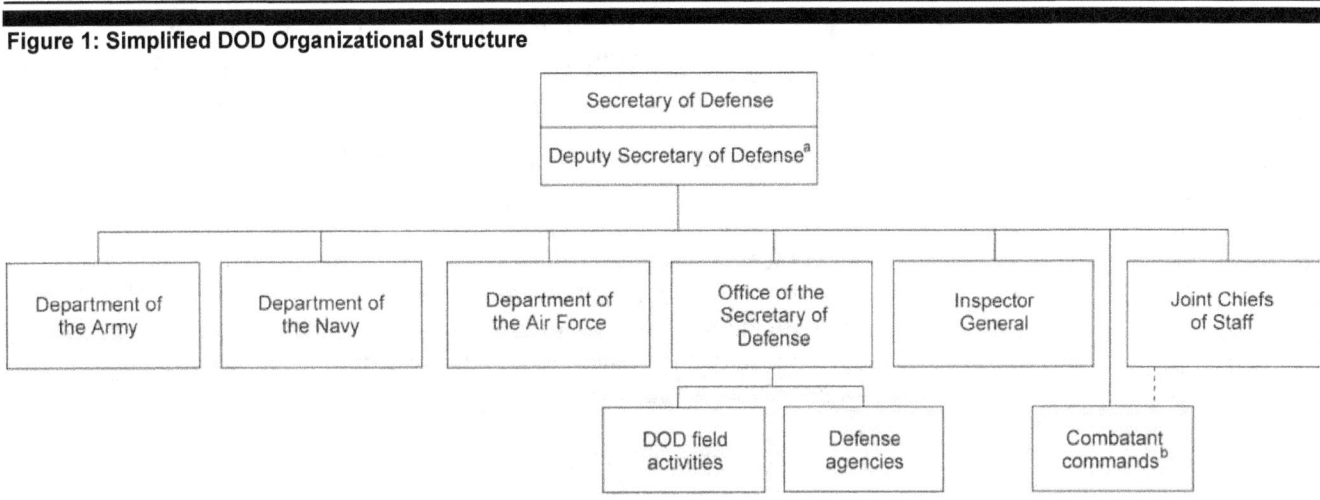

Source: GAO analysis based on DOD data.

[a]The Deputy Secretary of Defense serves as the DOD Chief Management Officer, who has responsibilities, under statutes and department guidance, related to improving the efficiency and effectiveness of business operations.

[b]The Chairman of the Joint Chiefs of Staff serves as the spokesperson for the commanders of the combatant commands, particularly for the operational requirements of the commands.

In support of its military operations, DOD performs an assortment of interrelated and interdependent business functions, such as logistics management, procurement, health care management, and financial management. As we have previously reported, the DOD systems environment that supports these business functions is overly complex and error prone, and is characterized by (1) little standardization across the department, (2) multiple systems performing the same tasks, (3) the same data stored in multiple systems, and (4) the need for data to be entered manually into multiple systems.[12] According to DOD's IT investment portfolio, for fiscal year 2011, the department allotted approximately $36.6 billion to operate, maintain, and modernize its IT systems. We have designated DOD's business systems modernization

---

[12]GAO, *Business Systems Modernization: DOD Continues to Improve Institutional Approach, but Further Steps Needed*, GAO-06-658 (Washington, D.C.: May 15, 2006) and *DOD Financial Management: Implementation Weaknesses in Army and Air Force Business Systems Could Jeopardize DOD's Auditability Goals*, GAO-12-134 (Washington, D.C.: Feb. 28, 2012).

GAO-13-311 Defense Major Automated Information Systems

program as high risk for the past 17 years, due to challenges in modernizing the department's business systems environment.[13]

DOD's Acquisition Guidance for MAIS Programs

Of the $36.6 billion allotted for DOD IT investments for fiscal year 2011, based on DOD's IT investment portfolio, at least $5.6 billion was for MAIS programs. The MAIS programs include a range of systems, such as communications systems, business systems (e.g., logistics management and financial management systems), and command and control systems, which are intended to provide department and component officials with easy access to information to effectively organize, plan, direct, and monitor mission operations.

MAIS programs must comply with one of two DOD acquisition frameworks. The first framework—referred to as the defense acquisition management system framework—was last updated in December 2008 and applies to all DOD IT acquisition programs except business system modernization programs that exceed $1 million in total costs.[14] The second framework—referred to as the business capability life-cycle acquisition model—was released in June 2011 and applies to all business system modernization programs with total costs exceeding $1 million.[15] The business system modernization programs are required to use this framework instead of the defense acquisition management system framework in an effort to address challenges previously experienced when implementing business systems, such as implementing solutions without fully understanding business needs.

The defense acquisition management system framework establishes the steps that programs should take as they plan, design, acquire, deploy, operate, and maintain their systems. Specifically, it consists of five program life-cycle phases and five related decision points, which are shown in figure 2 and described following the figure. The milestone decision authority for programs that comply with this framework is either the Under Secretary of Defense for Acquisition, Technology, and Logistics; the DOD component head; a component acquisition executive; or when authorized, a designee.

---

[13]GAO, *High-Risk Series: An Update*, GAO-11-278 (Washington, D.C.: February 2011).

[14]DOD Instruction 5000.02, *Operation of the Defense Acquisition System* (Dec. 8, 2008).

[15]Directive-Type Memorandum 11-009, *Acquisition Policy for Defense Business Systems (DBS)* (June 23, 2011).

Figure 2: Defense Acquisition Management System Framework

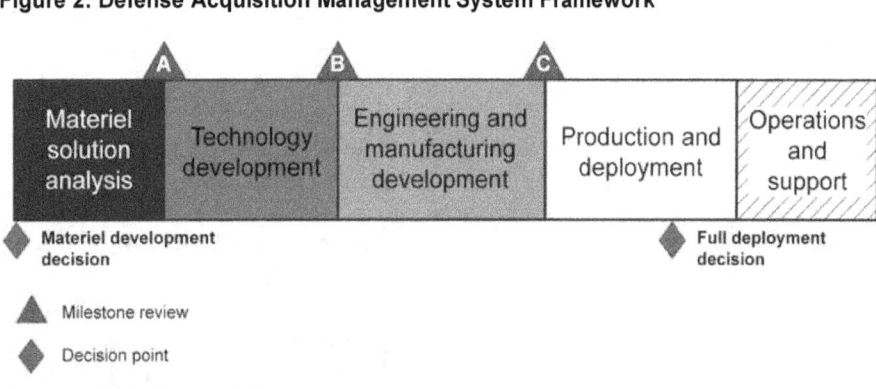

Source: GAO analysis based on DOD data.

- **Materiel solution analysis:** Refine the initial system solution (concept) and create a strategy for acquiring the solution. A decision is made at the end of this phase to authorize acquisition of the program—referred to as milestone A.

- **Technology development:** Determine the appropriate set of technologies to be integrated into the system solution while simultaneously refining user requirements. A decision is made at the end of this phase to authorize product development based on well-defined technology and a reasonable system design plan—referred to as milestone B. An APB is first established at the milestone B decision point.[16] A program's first APB contains the original life-cycle cost estimate, schedule estimate, and performance parameters that were approved for that program by the milestone decision authority. The first APB is established after the program has assessed the viability of various technologies and refined user requirements to identify the most appropriate technology solution that demonstrates that it can meet users' needs.

- **Engineering and manufacturing development:** Develop a system and demonstrate through developer testing that the system can function in its target environment. A decision is made at the end of this phase to authorize entry of the system into the production and

---

[16]An APB reflects the threshold and objective values for the minimum number of cost, schedule, and performance attributes that describe the program over its life cycle.

GAO-13-311 Defense Major Automated Information Systems

deployment phase or into limited deployment in support of operational testing—referred to as milestone C.

- **Production and deployment:** Achieve an operational capability that satisfies the mission needs, as verified through independent operational test and evaluation, and to implement the system at all applicable locations.

- **Operations and support:** Operationally sustain the system in the most cost-effective manner over its life cycle.

In addition to the three milestone decision points included in this framework (milestones A, B, and C), the framework also includes two other decision points: (1) materiel development decision, which authorizes officials to conduct analyses to assess the potential solutions that can satisfy the program's requirements, and (2) full deployment decision, which authorizes the system to be deployed to all remaining locations beyond limited fielding locations.[17]

In March 2009, the Defense Science Board reported that DOD's acquisition process for IT systems was too long, ineffective, and did not accommodate the rapid evolution of IT.[18] As such, the Board recommended that DOD develop new acquisition and requirements development processes for IT systems that would be agile, incremental, and allow requirements to be prioritized based on need and technical readiness. Subsequently, DOD developed a new framework—the business capability life-cycle acquisition model—that outlines the key steps that programs should take through the life cycle of acquisition of each major business system. This framework is intended to allow for more flexible acquisition processes that may be tailored to specific programs. Additionally, the framework is intended to address challenges that have previously impacted the delivery of IT business capabilities, such as programs lacking well-defined, strategically linked requirements, and transitioning too quickly from identifying a perceived business problem to implementing a specific solution. Specifically, this model

---

[17]Limited fielding is the deployment of a capability to a limited number of users to test the capability in an operational environment.

[18]Defense Science Board, *Report of the Defense Science Board Task Force on Department of Defense Policies and Procedures for the Acquisition of Information Technology* (Washington, D.C.: March 2009).

consists of seven program life-cycle phases and five milestone decision points, as shown in figure 3. The milestone decision authority for programs that are required to comply with this framework can either be the Under Secretary of Defense for Acquisition, Technology, and Logistics; the Deputy Chief Management Officer; the DOD Chief Information Officer; a component acquisition executive; or when authorized, a designee.

Figure 3: Business Capability Life-cycle Acquisition Model

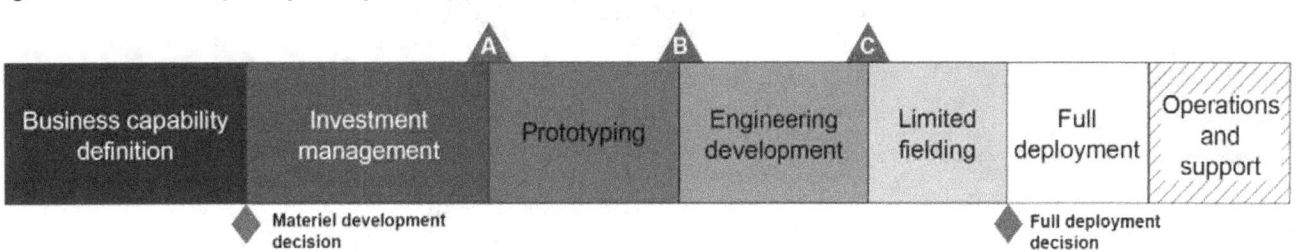

| Business capability definition | Investment management | Prototyping | Engineering development | Limited fielding | Full deployment | Operations and support |

Materiel development decision

Full deployment decision

▲ Milestone review/ milestone decision authority decision point

◆ Milestone decision authority decision point

Source: GAO analysis based on DOD data

Of these seven life-cycle phases, six are consistent with or similar to the five phases in the defense acquisition system framework (one of the phases in the defense acquisition system framework—production and deployment—corresponds to two phases in the business capability life-cycle model—limited fielding and full deployment). The seventh phase in the business capability life-cycle model is called business capability definition and occurs at the start of a program. The purpose of this phase is to analyze a perceived business problem or capability gap. This model also includes the five decision points included in the defense acquisition management framework—milestones A, B, and C, materiel development decision, and full deployment decision.

Statutory Requirements for MAIS Programs

In addition to adhering to one of two DOD acquisition frameworks, MAIS programs must also comply with annual and quarterly reporting requirements identified in statute.[19] In this regard, each calendar year, DOD must submit to Congress a report on each MAIS program, including information on the cost, schedule, and performance of the program.[20] Specifically, DOD must report, among other things, on each program's development and implementation schedules and development and full life-cycle cost estimates; and provide a summary of the key performance parameters for each program. It must also provide a summary of any major changes for each MAIS program.

Moreover, on a quarterly basis, the program manager for each MAIS program is required to provide the senior DOD official responsible for the program a report that identifies any variance in the program's cost, schedule, or performance.[21] Depending on the determination after reviewing the variance identified in the quarterly report, the senior DOD official must notify the congressional defense committees of any programs that have experienced either a significant or critical change, as described below:

- **Significant change.** A significant change must be declared if the program has experienced a schedule delay of more than 6 months but less than a year; estimated costs for the program have increased by at least 15 percent, but less than 25 percent; or there has been a significant adverse change in the expected performance of the system. If such an event occurs, the senior DOD official must notify the congressional defense committees in writing no later than 45 days after receiving the quarterly report from the program manager.

- **Critical change.** A critical change must be declared if the program failed to achieve a full deployment decision within 5 years after the milestone A decision or, if there was no milestone A decision, the date when the preferred alternative was selected for the program; experienced a schedule delay of more than 1 year; experienced an estimated development or full life-cycle cost increase of 25 percent or more over the original estimate; or experienced a change in the

---

[19]10 U.S.C. §§ 2445b and 2445c.

[20]10 U.S.C. § 2445b.

[21]10 U.S.C. § 2445c.

expected performance of the system that will undermine the ability of the system to perform as intended. If such an event occurs, the senior DOD official must carry out an evaluation of the program and submit a report to the congressional defense committees no later than 60 days after receiving the quarterly report from the program manager.

For programs that declare a critical change, the evaluation must assess the projected cost and schedule for completing the program if current requirements are not modified; assess the projected cost and schedule for completing the program based on a reasonable modification of requirements; and assess the rough order of magnitude of the cost and schedule for any reasonable alternative system or capability.

Best Practices for Managing IT Acquisition Programs

Entities such as the Software Engineering Institute at Carnegie Mellon University have developed best practices to help guide organizations to effectively plan and manage their acquisitions of major IT systems, such as the MAIS programs.[22] Our prior reviews have shown that proper implementation of such practices can significantly increase the likelihood of delivering promised system capabilities on time and within budget.[23] These practices include, but are not limited to:

- **Risk management:** A process for anticipating problems and taking appropriate steps to mitigate risks and minimize their impact on program commitments. It involves identifying and documenting risks, categorizing them based on their estimated impact, prioritizing them, developing risk mitigation strategies, and tracking progress in executing the strategies.

- **Requirements management:** Requirements establish what the system is to do, how well it is to do it, and how it is to interact with other systems. Effective management of requirements includes developing criteria for the evaluation and acceptance of requirements,

---

[22]Software Engineering Institute, *CMMI-ACQ*, version 1.3 (Pittsburgh, Penn., November 2010).

[23]See, for example, GAO, *Information Technology: Foundational Steps Being Taken to Make Needed FBI Systems Modernization Management Improvements*, GAO-04-842 (Washington, D.C.: Sept. 10, 2004) and *Information Technology: FBI Is Implementing Key Acquisition Methods on Its New Case Management System, but Related Agencywide Guidance Needs to Be Improved*, GAO-08-1014 (Washington, D.C.: Sept. 23, 2008).

obtaining commitments to requirements, and controlling requirements changes over the course of the program. It also ensures that requirements are validated against user needs and that each requirement traces back to the business need and forward to its design and testing.

- **Project monitoring and control:** Provides an understanding of the project's progress, so that appropriate corrective actions can be taken if performance deviates from plans. Effective practices in this area include monitoring program performance against the program plan, monitoring stakeholder involvement throughout the life of the program, and managing corrective actions to closure.

- **Independent verification and validation:** A process whereby organizations can reduce the risks inherent in system development and acquisition efforts by having a knowledgeable party who is independent of the developer determine that the system or product meets the users' needs and fulfills its intended purpose.

GAO Previously Reported on DOD's Challenges in Implementing Certain MAIS Programs

We have previously reported and made recommendations on DOD's efforts to implement certain MAIS programs.[24]

- In July 2007, we reported that the Army lacked certain processes to support oversight of its modernization of selected business systems.[25] For example, we noted that the Army did not have reliable processes, such as an IV&V function, to help support its oversight of the Global

---

[24]GAO, *DOD Financial Management: Implementation Weaknesses in Army and Air Force Business Systems Could Jeopardize DOD's Auditability Goals,* GAO-12-134 (Washington, D.C.: Feb. 28, 2012); *DOD Business Transformation: Improved Management Oversight of Business System Modernization Efforts Needed,* GAO-11-53 (Washington, D.C.: Oct. 7, 2010); *DOD Business Systems Modernization: Navy Implementing a Number of Key Management Controls on Enterprise Resource Planning System, but Improvements Still Needed,* GAO-09-841 (Washington, D.C.: Sept. 15, 2009); *DOD Business Systems Modernization: Important Management Controls Being Implemented on Major Navy Program, but Improvements Needed in Key Areas,* GAO-08-896 (Washington, D.C.: Sept. 8, 2008); *DOD Business Transformation: Air Force's Current Approach Increases Risk That Asset Visibility Goals and Transformation Priorities Will Not Be Achieved,* GAO-08-866 (Washington, D.C.: Aug. 8, 2008); and *DOD Business Transformation: Lack of an Integrated Strategy Puts the Army's Asset Visibility System Investments at Risk,* GAO-07-860 (Washington, D.C.: July 27, 2007).

[25]GAO-07-860.

Combat Support System (GCSS-Army) program. As a result, we recommended that the department establish an IV&V function for GCSS-Army that reports to Army management outside of the program office. DOD agreed with this recommendation and, in August 2009, awarded a contract to carry out an IV&V function for the GCSS-Army program.

- We also reported in August 2008 that the Air Force had not fully implemented best practices related to risk management and system testing for the Defense Enterprise Accounting and Management System (DEAMS) and Expeditionary Combat Support System (ECSS) programs.[26] Specifically, we found that program risks were monitored, overseen, and managed independently by various groups or activities within each of the programs without adequate visibility at the program management level. Additionally, DEAMS program officials acknowledged that nonstandardized computer desktop configurations represented a potential risk for system testing because the system might function differently in operating environments that were not the same as those in which the system was tested. We recommended that the program offices for DEAMS and ECSS (1) ensure that risk management activities at all levels of the program are identified and communicated to program management to facilitate oversight and monitoring, and (2) test their systems on relevant computer desktop configurations prior to deployment at a given location. DOD concurred with the recommendations and both program offices took appropriate action to address these recommendations.

- In September 2008, we reported that DOD had implemented key IT management controls on its Navy Enterprise Resource Planning (Navy ERP) program, but needed to make improvements in key areas.[27] We recommended that the department, among other things, take action to (1) increase the quality of the program's integrated master schedule, (2) improve the reliability of Navy ERP's cost estimates, and (3) improve Navy ERP's management of program risks. Further, in September 2009, we noted that the program still needed to improve key management controls.[28] At that time, we

---

[26] GAO-08-866.

[27] GAO-08-896.

[28] GAO-09-841.

recommended that the department take steps to (1) improve its change control process and (2) increase the value of the Navy ERP IV&V function. DOD generally concurred with the recommendations in both reports and took actions to implement the recommendations.

- We also found that the cost and schedule estimates for DEAMS, ECSS, and GCSS-Army did not fully follow best practices for developing reliable cost and schedule estimates, as highlighted in our October 2010 report.[29] As a result, we recommended that the ECSS and GCSS-Army program offices update their cost estimates to include best practices, such as using actual costs and preparing a sensitivity analysis. Further, we recommended that the DEAMS, ECSS, and GCSS-Army program offices develop integrated master schedules that fully incorporate best practices, such as capturing and sequencing all activities. In addition to these program-specific findings and recommendations, we reported that DOD lacked a comprehensive set of performance measures to assess these systems and their contributions to transforming business operations. We therefore recommended that DOD's chief management officer and the chief management officers for each military department establish performance measures based on quantitative data that would enable the department to assess whether each respective military service's modernization efforts are providing the intended business capabilities to the system users. DOD concurred with our recommendations and stated that it planned to take action to implement them, where applicable. Subsequently, the DEAMS program updated its integrated master schedule. A separate GAO review is ongoing to determine the reliability of this schedule. Additionally, at the end of 2012, the GCSS-Army program completed updating its integrated master schedule. In 2013, we plan to conduct a study to, among other things, determine the reliability of this updated schedule.

- In February 2012, we reported on deficiencies in the capabilities of ECSS, DEAMS, and GCSS-Army to perform essential functions as intended.[30] We noted, among other things, that independent assessments of each system had identified operational problems with these systems. Accordingly, we recommended that the milestone decision authorities for these programs ensure that future system

---

[29]GAO-11-53.

[30]GAO-12-134.

GAO-13-311 Defense Major Automated Information Systems

deficiencies identified through independent assessments be resolved or mitigated prior to further deployment of the systems. DOD officials subsequently stated that the Air Force was aggressively working to resolve DEAMS's deficiencies. Additionally, we reported that certain users of DEAMS were having difficulties in using the system to perform their day-to-day operations. Thus, we recommended that the Air Force establish time lines and monitor the status of the corrective actions to help ensure the issues identified by these users were resolved in a timely manner. DOD officials stated that they had also taken steps to address this recommendation, such as implementing oversight bodies to ensure all issues are identified and resolved or mitigated in a timely manner.

- We also reported in October 2012 that DOD's chief information officer rated DEAMS and GCSS-Army as low or moderately low risk on the Office of Management and Budget's IT Dashboard from July 2009 through March 2012,[31] even though we reported that both programs had experienced cost increases and schedule delays.[32] As such, we recommended that DOD ensure that its chief information officer ratings reflect available investment performance assessments. DOD concurred with our recommendation and stated that it would update its chief information officer ratings process to better report risk and improve timeliness and transparency.

---

[31]GAO, *Information Technology Dashboard: Opportunities Exist to Improve Transparency and Oversight of Investment Risk at Select Agencies*, GAO-13-98 (Washington, D.C.: Oct. 16, 2012). The IT Dashboard is a public website that provides detailed information on federal agencies' major IT investments, including assessments of actual performance against cost and schedule targets.

[32]GAO, *DOD Financial Management: Reported Status of Department of Defense's Enterprise Resource Planning Systems*, GAO-12-565R (Washington, D.C.: Mar. 30, 2012) and GAO-11-53.

Large Variations Exist among Selected Programs in Staying within Cost and Schedule Estimates and Meeting System Performance Targets

Among the 14 MAIS programs selected for our study, there were large variations in the extent to which programs were staying within cost and schedule estimates and meeting system performance targets. Specifically, 9 stayed within their planned cost estimates, while 5 did not; 5 programs remained on schedule, while 9 experienced delays; and 8 programs met their system performance targets, while 5 did not fully meet their targets and 1 did not have system performance data available. When looking at the data collectively, 3 programs—Air Force's Financial Information Resource System (FIRST), Information Transport Services (ITS) Increment 1, and the Defense Information Systems Agency's (DISA) Global Combat Support System-Joint (GCSS-J) Increment 7—stayed within their planned cost and schedule estimates and met their system performance targets. Two of the 14 programs—Navy ERP and Air Force's ECSS—experienced shortcomings in all three of the areas—cost, schedule, and performance. Program profiles with cost, schedule, and system performance details on each of the selected programs are included in appendix II. Table 1 provides a summary of the cost, schedule, and performance results for the 14 selected programs.

Table 1: Summary of Cost, Schedule, and Performance Results for the Selected Programs

Component/ Program	Stayed within planned cost estimate	Exceeded planned cost estimate	Stayed within planned schedule estimate	Exceeded planned schedule estimate	Met system performance targets	Did not fully meet system performance targets
Air Force						
DEAMS Increment 1	✓		✓			✓
ECSS Increment 1		✓ᵃ		✓ᵃ		✓
FIRST	✓		✓		✓	
ITS Increment 1	✓		✓		✓	
Mission Planning Systems (MPS) Increment 4	✓			✓		✓
Army						
GCSS-Army	✓			✓	✓	
Global Command and Control System – Army (GCCS-A) Block 4	✓			✓	✓	
Tactical Mission Command (TMC)		✓	✓		✓	
DISA						
GCSS-J Increment 7	✓		✓		✓	
Teleport Generation 3ᵇ		✓		✓		
Navy						
Common Aviation Command and Control System (CAC2S) Increment 1		✓		✓	✓	
Consolidated Afloat Networks and Enterprise Services (CANES)	✓			✓		✓ᶜ
Distributed Common Ground System – Navy (DCGS-N) Increment 1	✓			✓	✓	
Navy ERP		✓		✓		✓
Total	9	5	5	9	8	5

Source: GAO analysis of data provided by DOD officials.

ᵃECSS had not established an APB. As such, we compared its latest cost and schedule estimates against its initial estimates.

ᵇAs of December 2012, Teleport Generation 3 was in the early stages of implementation and had not fully implemented any terminals; as such, there were no system performance data available.

ᶜCANES conducted performance tests in a lab environment prior to milestone C. According to program officials, known limitations of the tests were documented and will be evaluated in subsequent testing prior to a full deployment decision.

Nine of the Selected Programs Stayed within Their Planned Total Life-cycle Cost Estimates, While the Remaining Five Did Not

Nine of the 14 selected programs stayed within their planned total life-cycle cost estimates. Specifically, when comparing these programs' latest total life-cycle cost estimates to their first APB estimates, 8 of these 9 programs reduced their cost estimates and 1 remained consistent.

- Six of the nine programs reduced their planned total life-cycle cost estimates due to lower than expected contract costs, implementation of new technology that cost less, program budget cuts, or transferring costs to another DOD program. For example, as of September 2012, the latest life-cycle cost estimate for Navy's DCGS-N Increment 1 program had decreased about 10 percent from its first APB estimate (from approximately $1.43 billion down to about $1.28 billion) due, in part, to lower than expected costs associated with software development. Additionally, as of November 2012, the latest life-cycle cost estimate for the Air Force's ITS Increment 1 program had decreased about 10 percent (from approximately $3.8 billion down to about $3.4 billion). ITS officials attributed the decrease primarily to contractors' proposals being about 40 percent lower than what the program office expected based on past proposals. Further, as of September 2012, the latest life-cycle cost estimate for DISA's GCSS-J program had decreased about 17 percent from the program's first APB estimate (from about $210 million down to approximately $173 million) due to program budget cuts. Program officials stated that the program's incremental development approach had enabled them to absorb the budget cuts because the approach allowed requirements to be reprioritized and developed based on available funding.

- Two of the nine programs—the Air Force's MPS Increment 4 and FIRST—experienced decreases in their planned total life-cycle cost estimates due to significant reductions in scope or functionality. For example, the planned total life-cycle costs for MPS decreased 53 percent when the program terminated originally planned developments and upgrades for 10 of the 18 aircraft. According to program officials, this decision was made because the program was experiencing significant schedule slippages and the Air Force had other funding priorities. Additionally, the planned total life-cycle costs for FIRST decreased about 19 percent because only one legacy system was replaced, rather than the three that were originally planned. Specifically, program officials stated that a gap analysis conducted after the award of FIRST's development contract revealed that the requirements baseline was missing key functions needed to replace the two additional legacy systems.

- Lastly, as of September 2012, the total life-cycle cost estimate for the Air Force's DEAMS was consistent with its first APB estimate of $1.4 billion, which was recently established in February 2012. However, it is important to note that the program spent approximately $334 million and took 9 years before it established its APB. In other words, the program had been underway for almost a decade before it had developed a robust estimate for how much the program was expected to ultimately cost. DEAMS officials attributed the delays in developing the APB, in part, to the complexity of reengineering business processes; evolving technical requirements; and designing, developing, and testing the software.

Five of the 14 selected programs experienced increases in their planned total life-cycle cost estimates ranging from 3 to 578 percent.

- The latest life-cycle cost estimate for the Navy's CAC2S Increment 1 program increased 578 percent from its first APB estimate of $347 million in August 2000 to $2.4 billion as of September 2012. Program officials attributed the cost increase to the addition of new requirements for two additional Navy command and support centers, which also required the development of additional systems, and related costs that were added to the program in 2002.

- The latest life-cycle cost estimate for Navy ERP increased about 31 percent from the program's first APB estimate of approximately $2.0 billion in August 2004 to $2.6 billion as of September 2012. Program officials attributed this program's cost increases to schedule slippages that occurred in September 2009 and August 2011, an increase in demand for on-site support and stabilization activities during system deployments, and the need to add requirements to support business process reengineering and improve financial management information.

- The latest life-cycle cost estimate (as of September 2012) for the Army's TMC program had increased 6 percent from the program's first APB estimate of about $1.97 billion in February 2008, to $2.1 billion. Program officials attributed the cost increase, in part, to several scope increases that the Army made, including the addition of new technology into the program baseline.

- The latest life-cycle cost estimate (as of September 2012) for DISA's Teleport Generation 3 program increased nominally by 3 percent from its first APB of $563.7 million in September 2010 to about $581.2 million. Teleport officials attributed this increase, in part, to a more rigorous and accurate projection of operations and maintenance costs and a 3-year extension of the program's planned operations and maintenance phase.

- The fifth program that experienced an increase in its cost estimate was the Air Force's ECSS.[33] The program's initial cost estimate from June 2005 (which was based on limited information about the program's requirements and the viability of technologies available to meet the program's needs) was $3 billion, while the program's latest life-cycle cost estimate as of February 2011 (also based on limited program information) was about $3.2 billion—an approximately 7 percent increase. In December 2012, the Air Force decided to cancel ECSS due to its significant schedule delays, poor system and contractor performance, and changing requirements.

Table 2 provides a summary of the percent of cost increase or decrease from each selected program's first APB estimates to their latest planned total life-cycle cost estimates.

---

[33]ECSS had not established an APB. As such, the 7 percent represents the increase from the program's initial estimate (as of June 2005) to its latest estimate (as of February 2011).

Table 2: Changes in Selected Programs' First APB Estimates and Latest Planned Total Life-cycle Cost Estimates

Component	Program	Percent change in life-cycle cost estimate since first APB (%)
Air Force	DEAMS Increment 1	0%
	ECSS Increment 1	↑ 7[a]
	FIRST	↓ 19
	ITS Increment 1	↓ 10
	MPS Increment 4	↓ 53
Army	GCSS-Army	↓ 1
	GCCS-A Block 4	↓ 43
	TMC	↑ 6
DISA	GCSS-J Increment 7	↓ 17
	Teleport Generation 3	↑ 3
Navy	CAC2S Increment 1	↑ 578
	CANES	↓ 7
	DCGS-N Increment 1	↓ 10
	Navy ERP	↑ 31

Source: GAO analysis of data provided by DOD officials.

[a]ECSS had not established an APB. As such, the 7 percent represents the increase from the program's initial estimate (as of June 2005) to its latest estimate (as of February 2011).

Five of the Selected Programs Stayed within Their Schedule Estimates, While the Remaining Nine Experienced Schedule Slippages

The latest schedule estimates for 5 of the 14 selected programs remained consistent with each program's respective first APB schedule estimates. Specifically, each of the key milestones established in the first APBs for the Air Force's DEAMS, FIRST, and ITS; the Army's TMC; and DISA's GCSS-J had not changed when compared to the milestone dates in these programs' latest schedules. For example, TMC's latest schedule (as of September 2012) estimated that the program would be fully deployed in September 2018, which is consistent with the program's first APB. While the DEAMS program had not experienced a schedule slippage from its first APB—recently established in February 2012—as previously mentioned, the program took almost 9 years to establish its first APB.

Nine of the 14 selected programs had experienced slippages in their planned schedule estimates, ranging from a few months to 10 years. One of the 9 programs—CANES—had experienced a significant slippage in its schedule, with an 11-month delay in meeting its planned date to obtain approval to begin limited deployment of the system (referred to as milestone C). Six programs had experienced critical slippages of more than 1 year.[34] For example,

- CAC2S experienced a 10-year slippage in its full deployment date—currently scheduled for September 2018. Program officials attributed this delay, in part, to the addition of new requirements in 2002 and problems with one of its contractors, which the CAC2S program office determined was unable to develop a solution that met the program's requirements.

- MPS experienced a 3-year slippage in its full deployment decision date—currently scheduled for May 2013. Program officials stated that the slippage was due, in part, to the complexity of developing, integrating, and testing mission planning capabilities.

- Compared to its first APB schedule, GCSS-Army experienced a 10-month slippage in its full deployment decision date—which occurred in December 2012. GCSS-Army officials attributed the slippage to the discovery of configuration problems related to scalability of the system, which resulted in the need to make design corrections. GCSS-Army also experienced a 2-year slippage in its full deployment date—currently scheduled for the fourth quarter of fiscal year 2017. Officials attributed this delay to a change in scope to include both tactical and installation warehouses to support DOD's statutory requirement for auditability by fiscal year 2017.

- Although ECSS had not established an APB schedule before it was canceled, the program had experienced multiple slippages compared to its initial schedule. For example, its planned date to obtain approval to begin development of the system (referred to as milestone B) had slipped 5 years—from the end of fiscal year 2007 to December 2012—when the program was canceled.

---

[34]Thresholds for significant and critical change designations were established in 10 U.S.C. § 2445c.

Table 3 provides a summary of the slippages experienced by the selected MAIS programs when compared to each program's first APB.

Table 3: Selected MAIS Programs' Schedule Slippages Compared to First APB Schedules

Component	Program	Schedule slippage since first APB (slipped milestone)
Air Force	DEAMS Increment 1	None
	ECSS Increment 1	5 years (milestone B)[a]
	FIRST	None
	ITS Increment 1	None
	MPS Increment 4	3 years (full deployment decision)
Army	GCSS-Army	2 years (full deployment)
	GCCS-A Block 4	3 years (full deployment)
	TMC	None
DISA	GCSS-J Increment 7	None
	Teleport Generation 3	6 months (full deployment decision)
Navy	CAC2S Increment 1	10 years (full deployment)
	CANES	11 months (milestone C)
	DCGS-N Increment 1	6 months (limited deployment decision)
	Navy ERP	2 years (full deployment)

Source: GAO analysis of data provided by DOD officials.

[a]ECSS did not establish an APB before it was canceled in December 2012. Therefore, the 5-year delay in achieving milestone B represents a comparison of the program's initial schedule estimate to its latest estimate.

As reflected in table 4, program officials attributed the schedule slippages for the nine programs to numerous causes, ranging from increased scope to contractor performance problems.

Table 4: Causes for Schedule Slippages Among Nine Selected Programs

Program	Increased scope	Unanticipated requirements or unplanned work	Dependence on other DOD programs	System performance problems	Contractor performance problems	Bid protest	Under-estimating software development complexity	Delay in fiscal year 2011 budget
CAC2S Increment 1	✓				✓			
CANES						✓		✓
DCGS-N Increment 1			✓					
ECSS Increment 1					✓	✓		
GCCS-A Block 4	✓		✓					
GCSS-Army	✓	✓						
MPS Increment 4		✓		✓			✓	
Navy ERP		✓		✓				
Teleport Generation 3			✓					
Total	**3**	**3**	**3**	**2**	**2**	**2**	**1**	**1**

Source: GAO analysis of data provided by DOD officials.

Further discussion of the specific causes for schedule slippages among the nine programs is included in appendix II.

Eight of the Selected Programs Reported Meeting System Performance Targets, While Five Did Not Fully Meet Targets, and One Did Not Have System Performance Data Available

Eight of the 14 selected programs reported meeting their system performance targets. These programs were the Air Force's FIRST and ITS; the Army's GCCS-A, GCSS-Army, and TMC; DISA's GCSS-J; and the Navy's CAC2S and DCGS-N. For example, TMC reported that it met all three of its key performance parameters in fiscal year 2012, which include supporting net-centric military operations and displaying unified information on subject matters, such as friendly forces and enemy forces. Additionally, as of September 2012, the ITS program reported that it was meeting all four of its performance measures related to interoperability, availability, support, and reliability. In another example, in June 2012, the Army's Test and Evaluation Command reported that GCSS-Army release 1.1 was operationally effective, operationally suitable, and survivable against cyber threats. One program—Teleport—did not have system performance data available because, as of December 2012, the program was in the early stages of implementation and no terminals were fully implemented.

On the other hand, 5 of the 14 selected programs reported experiencing system performance problems, which resulted in these systems not performing as intended and reducing the value of the systems. These performance problems included the existence of many defects in an operational system; not meeting system interoperability, maintainability, or processing time targets; and an inability to demonstrate that system requirements were met. For example, a 2010 operational assessment of DEAMS identified 350 must-fix deficiencies that impaired this system's ability to perform essential functions at its deployed sites and diminished the system's efficiency and effectiveness in accounting for business transactions and reporting reliable financial information. A follow-up operational assessment by the Air Force's Test and Evaluation Center in 2012 identified 210 new deficiencies in DEAMS and 15 repeat deficiencies from 2010. Also, as of October 2012, for DEAMS's 38 performance metrics, the program had identified 11 as needing attention and 12 that had significant concerns.

Additionally, in 2011, operational testing of MPS by the Air Force's Test and Evaluation Center identified significant system defects in one of the program's aircraft developments and upgrades, which impaired MPS's ability to perform certain system functions. Subsequently, the program developed patches intended to address many of the deficiencies. In November 2012, program officials stated that the Air Force's Test and Evaluation Center was conducting operational tests to determine whether the previously identified deficiencies had been corrected. As of December 2012, the results of these tests were not yet known. Additionally, in September 2010, a significant number of system deficiencies were identified in the Navy ERP system. As of December 2012, certain deficiencies had been resolved. However, Navy ERP officials reported that 560 system defects remained open and that the program was continuing to address those deficiencies.

Further, in July 2012, performance tests that were conducted on CANES in a lab environment showed that 23 of 69 system requirements could not be fully demonstrated in the development model. According to the test report, these requirements were not fully met primarily due to: (1) constraints of testing in the laboratory environment, which could not simulate certain conditions required on vessels, such as wireless connectivity, which was not available in the lab due to security concerns; (2) testing on a development model, which did not represent the final production model; (3) a limited schedule—the test period was 343 hours, but the reliability threshold is 495 hours; and (4) testing with only two hosted applications while CANES is expected to host many applications. Table 5 identifies the system performance problems for the five programs.

Table 5: System Performance Problems among the Five Programs

| Component | Program | Types of performance problems | | |
		System deficiencies	Unmet system performance measures	Certain system requirements not fully demonstrated
Air Force	DEAMS Increment 1	✓	✓	
	ECSS Increment 1	✓		
	MPS Increment 4	✓		
Navy	CANES			✓
	Navy ERP	✓	✓	
	Total	**4**	**2**	**1**

Source: GAO analysis of data provided by DOD officials.

Selected Programs Demonstrated Mixed Results in Effectively Defining and Managing Risks of Various Levels

According to CMMI-ACQ, an effective risk management process identifies potential problems before they occur, so that risk-handling activities may be planned and invoked, as needed, across the life of the project in order to mitigate adverse impacts on achieving objectives. Specifically, key risk management practices include:

- identifying risks, threats, and vulnerabilities that could negatively affect work efforts;

- evaluating and categorizing each identified risk using defined risk categories and parameters, such as likelihood and consequence, and determining each risk's relative priority;

- developing risk mitigation plans for selected risks to proactively reduce the potential impact of risk occurrence; and

- monitoring the status of each risk periodically and implementing the risk mitigation plan as appropriate.

CANES	The Navy had implemented these practices as part of its risk management for CANES.

- **Identify risks, threats, and vulnerabilities that could negatively affect work efforts.** The CANES program had identified risks, threats, and vulnerabilities that could negatively affect work efforts. In particular, as of November 2012, key risks as identified by the program office included: the possibility of uncovering significant integration issues during application integration testing due to insufficient testing time and test equipment, and the possibility of missing the full deployment decision date in December 2013 due to schedule slippage in testing.

- **Evaluate and categorize each identified risk using defined risk categories and parameters, such as likelihood and consequence, and determine each risk's relative priority.** The program had evaluated and categorized its risks based on probability and impact. For example, the program reported that the first key risk above had a "medium" exposure rating (meaning it may cause some increase in cost, disruption of schedule, or degradation of performance) and that the second risk had a "high" exposure rating (meaning it is likely to cause a significant increase in cost, disruption of schedule, or degradation of performance).

- **Develop risk mitigation plans for selected risks to proactively reduce the potential impact of risk occurrence.** CANES had developed mitigation plans to proactively reduce the potential impact of risk occurrence. For example, risk mitigation plans for the two aforementioned key risks included extending the application integration testing work schedule to 6 days per week to provide more sufficient testing time and purchasing additional testing equipment to eliminate the need to reconfigure the test equipment after its initial usage; and working with the testing community to expedite test reporting time lines prior to full deployment decision.

- **Monitor the status of each risk periodically and implement the risk mitigation plan as appropriate.** The program monitored its risks and documented the status of risk mitigation actions that had been taken, as well as new mitigation steps that had been developed since the prior month. For example, in May 2012, CANES had identified seven mitigation steps for one of its risks. In September 2012, the program had completed one of the mitigation steps and removed it from the mitigation plan.

In taking these actions, the CANES program had established and utilized effective risk management practices. Doing so should better position the program to mitigate adverse impacts from potential problems before they occur.

DEAMS

The Air Force had taken steps to implement certain risk management practices for DEAMS, but it had not periodically monitored the status of each risk and the program's risk reports were out of date and had not been regularly updated to include the current status of actions taken to mitigate risks. However, the program office recently took steps to update its risks and associated mitigation plans.

- **Identify risks, threats, and vulnerabilities that could negatively affect work efforts.** The DEAMS program had identified risks, threats, and vulnerabilities that could negatively affect work efforts. However, the program's risk reports were out of date, and risks and associated mitigation plans were not always assessed on a monthly basis. According to DEAMS program officials, in 2012 the program office diverted attention from other program management activities, including risk management, in order to fix a significant number of deficiencies identified during a 2010 operational assessment of the system. As a result, the program's approach to managing and mitigating risks became reactive, rather than proactive. In May 2012, a new DEAMS program manager was hired and directed the program to revamp its approach to risk management. Specifically, program officials reassessed and validated the risks, and developed new plans for mitigating them—which was recently completed in December 2012. Additionally, in September 2012, the program initiated a risk and issues working group that was to be responsible for approving and executing risk response plans. At the conclusion of our study, DEAMS provided its revalidated program risks and mitigation plans, as of December 2012. Collectively, these actions should help ensure that the program is properly identifying and managing its program risks.

- **Evaluate and categorize each identified risk using defined risk categories and parameters, such as likelihood and consequence, and determine each risk's relative priority.** The program had evaluated and categorized its identified risks. However, as stated previously, these risks were out of date and the program had recently taken steps to reassess and validate its risks.

- **Develop risk mitigation plans for selected risks to proactively reduce the potential impact of risk occurrence.** The program had developed mitigation plans for its identified risks. However, as stated previously, these risks and mitigations plans were out of date, and the program had recently taken steps to develop new mitigation plans for its risks.

- **Monitor the status of each risk periodically and implement the risk mitigation plan as appropriate.** As stated previously, as of November 2012, the program's risks were out of date, and the program had recently taken steps to improve its risk management process, including reassessing and validating its risks.

GCSS-Army

The Army also had implemented key risk management practices for GCSS-Army, but the program was using multiple risk management systems that contained inconsistent data.

- **Identify risks, threats, and vulnerabilities that could negatively affect work efforts.** The GCSS-Army program had identified risks, threats, and vulnerabilities that could negatively affect work efforts. However, the program lacked a centralized risk management system that maintained an up-to-date log of all current and relevant risks. Instead, the program's key risk management entities—including the GCSS-Army government program office, Army Enterprise Systems Integration Program office,[35] the system integrator contractor, and the IV&V contractor—each maintained separate risk management systems. Program officials stated that they only synchronize the risks from each of these sources on a quarterly basis. This approach was identified as problematic in September 2011 and again in October 2012 by GCSS-Army's IV&V contractor. Specifically, the contractor stated that the program's risk management process included multiple sources for tracking and managing risk information, and that these sources did not exchange information with each other. For example, as of December 2012, one of the top GCSS-Army risks that was presented at the December 2012 Risk Management Board meeting was not included in the GCSS-Army government program office's risk log that was provided to us. In discussing this omission, GCSS-Army

---

[35]The Army Enterprise Systems Integration Program integrates business processes and systems for the Army's logistics and financial ERP business systems, including GCSS-Army, the General Fund Enterprise Business System, and the Logistics Modernization Program.

officials stated that this was an oversight by the program management office and that the risk should have been included in the government program office's risk log. However, errors are more likely to occur when managing to multiple inconsistent risk management systems.

GCSS-Army officials stated that they did not want to implement a risk management process that would use a single system to track risks because the government and system integrator have separately identified risks with sensitive information that they do not communicate with each other. However, managing to multiple sets of inconsistent risk data can be counterproductive and increases the likelihood that risks are not being appropriately mitigated. Until GCSS-Army establishes a risk management system which ensures that the program has at least one comprehensive risk log that maintains an aggregation of all up-to-date risks and associated mitigations plans, GCSS-Army will lack assurance that it is appropriately mitigating all program risks and avoiding the likelihood that those risks materialize into program issues.

- **Evaluate and categorize each identified risk using defined risk categories and parameters, such as likelihood and consequence, and determine each risk's relative priority.** The program had categorized and prioritized its risks. Specifically, GCSS-Army assessed the likelihood and consequence of its risks based on criteria defined in its risk management plan, and ranked these risks in order of priority. For example, in the system integrator's September 2012 risk log, 3 of the top 10 risks were categorized as high risk, 3 were categorized as medium risk, and 4 were categorized as low risk.

- **Develop risk mitigation plans for selected risks to proactively reduce the potential impact of risk occurrence.** GCSS-Army had developed and implemented risk mitigation plans for its risks. Specifically, the program office's risk log, the Army Enterprise Systems Integration Program office's risk log, and the system integrator's risk log each outlined mitigation steps for their associated risks.

- **Monitor the status of each risk periodically and implement the risk mitigation plan as appropriate.** In its monthly risk logs, the program documented the mitigation steps for each risk listed, the status of any actions taken to implement the steps, as well as any new mitigation steps developed since the prior month. However, as stated earlier, the program lacked a centralized risk management system to maintain an up-to-date log of all current mitigation plans.

Selected Programs Showed Varied Progress in Applying IT Acquisition Best Practices

CANES, DEAMS, and GCSS-Army demonstrated varied progress in implementing IT acquisition best practices for requirements management and project monitoring and control. Specifically, CANES and GCSS-Army were implementing requirements management best practices. However, while DEAMS was implementing many requirements management best practices, the program did not trace all of its lower-level requirements to its higher-level system capabilities. The program's plan to map the remaining requirements by the fourth quarter of fiscal year 2013 should help address this deficiency. Regarding project monitoring and control, CANES had implemented effective best practices in this area. However, while DEAMS and GCSS-Army had implemented selected project monitoring and control best practices, DEAMS had experienced frequent turnover in its program manager position and GCSS-Army was not appropriately using its IV&V contractor. Until DEAMS and GCSS-Army address the gaps in their acquisition management practices, these programs may be at risk of not meeting planned cost and schedule milestones, and may implement systems that do not fully meet user needs.

CANES and GCSS-Army Had Implemented the Requirements Management Best Practices; DEAMS Had Implemented Most of Them, and Had Plans to Address Requirements Mapping Deficiencies

Requirements management is the process for ensuring that the system requirements are traceable, verifiable, and controlled. Traceability refers to the ability to follow a requirement from origin to implementation and is critical to understanding the interconnections and dependencies among the individual requirements and the impact when a requirement is changed. According to CMMI-ACQ, key practices in managing requirements include:

- establishing criteria for identifying appropriate requirements providers;

- establishing objective criteria for the evaluation and acceptance of requirements;

- assessing the impact of requirements on existing commitments;

- reviewing project plans, activities, and work products to ensure that they are consistent with the defined requirements; and

- ensuring traceability between the requirements and work products.[36]

CANES

The Navy had implemented CMMI best practices for managing CANES requirements.

- **Establish criteria for identifying appropriate requirements providers.** The program had established criteria for identifying appropriate requirements providers. Specifically, the program's requirements management plan identified specific roles and responsibilities for the entities that were to identify and maintain requirements.

- **Establish objective criteria for the evaluation and acceptance of requirements.** CANES had established a checklist of criteria for evaluating and accepting new requirements. The checklist included, for example, specifications for how a requirement must be worded before it would be accepted.

- **Assess the impact of requirements on existing commitments.** The program had assessed the impact of requirements on existing commitments. For example, the program had evaluated and documented how CANES's costs, schedule, and performance might be impacted by changes to requirements.

- **Review project plans, activities, and work products to ensure that they are consistent with the defined requirements.** The program reviewed project plans, activities, and work products to ensure that they were consistent with the defined requirements. For example, in May 2012, the program updated its plan for installing the CANES system on ships based on the program's progress to date and vessel availability.

- **Ensure traceability between the requirements and work products.** The program maintained traceability between its requirements and work products. For example, the program had

[36]CMMI-ACQ, Version 1.3 (November 2010).

traced each requirement in its requirements traceability matrix to the program's desired capabilities and technical baselines.

As a result, the CANES program had established effective requirements management practices, which should increase the likelihood that the program delivers a system that contains functionality that meets users' needs.

DEAMS

While the Air Force had implemented a number of requirements management best practices for DEAMS, it did not maintain complete traceability of all of its requirements and work products. Program officials stated that they plan to complete the mapping of DEAMS's outstanding requirements by the fourth quarter of fiscal year 2013.

- **Establish criteria for identifying appropriate requirements providers.** DEAMS had established criteria for distinguishing appropriate requirements providers. Specifically, the program's requirements management plan identified roles and responsibilities for the entities that were to identify and maintain requirements.

- **Establish objective criteria for the evaluation and acceptance of requirements.** DEAMS had established criteria for evaluating and accepting requirements. Specifically, prior to accepting a new requirement, program officials were expected to evaluate the requirement based on potential impacts to the business or operation, technical baseline, schedule, security, and finances.

- **Assess the impact of requirements on existing commitments.** DEAMS assessed whether new requirements would impact existing commitments. For example, during a system requirements review, the system integrator determined that the program contained more requirements than originally planned, and that, as a result, the program may be challenged to meet the program's schedule.

- **Review project plans, activities, and work products to ensure that they are consistent with the defined requirements.** The program had reviewed its project plan and work products to ensure consistency with requirements. For example, the program's system requirements document identified changes and additions made to the requirements.

- **Ensure traceability between the requirements and work products.** The program did not maintain complete traceability of all of its requirements and work products. Specifically, while the program had mapped each of its higher-level capabilities to its associated lower-level requirements, the program had not completed its mapping of each of its lower-level requirements to a higher-level capability. As such, the program was unable to ensure that all of the 1,998 requirements that were included in the system during its technology demonstration would be included in the upcoming releases of the system. Program officials stated that they expect this mapping to be completed by the fourth quarter of fiscal year 2013. The planned complete mapping of all of DEAMS's lower-level requirements to its higher-level capabilities should help ensure that the system is deployed with all of the intended functionality.

GCSS-Army

The Army had implemented requirements management best practices for the GCSS-Army program.

- **Establish criteria for identifying appropriate requirements providers.** GCSS-Army had established criteria for identifying appropriate requirements providers. Specifically, program officials identified criteria that specified five main sources of new requirements, including that the Assistant Secretary of the Army Financial Management and Comptroller is to provide financial management requirements.

- **Establish objective criteria for the evaluation and acceptance of requirements.** The program established criteria for the evaluation and acceptance of its requirements. For example, in evaluating and accepting new requirements, GCSS-Army's Configuration Control Board reviewed change request documentation, which included, among other things, a description of the change, the reason for the change, and potential impacts (e.g., organizational, technical) to the program.

- **Assess the impact of requirements on existing commitments.** GCSS-Army assessed the impact of requirements on existing commitments. Specifically, requests to make changes to requirements included an impact analysis that identified how the change may impact existing commitments.

- **Review project plans, activities, and work products to ensure that they are consistent with the defined requirements.** The program ensured that project plans and work products were consistent with requirements and changes made to them. For example, when GCSS-Army added new requirements to meet the mandate for auditability by fiscal year 2017, it extended its schedule to accommodate those requirements.

- **Ensure traceability between the requirements and work products.** GCSS-Army ensured traceability between its requirements and work products by tracing its approved requirements (capabilities) from the program's Capability Production Document to the associated test procedures that were used to validate whether a developed capability performed as required.

By taking these steps, the GCSS-Army program demonstrated that it had established essential requirements management practices, which should increase the likelihood of the program delivering a system that contains functionality that meets users' needs.

CANES Implemented Project Monitoring and Control Practices, While DEAMS and GCSS-Army Lacked Certain Practices

According to CMMI-ACQ, an effective project monitoring and control process provides oversight of the program's performance, in order to allow appropriate corrective actions if actual performance deviates significantly from planned performance. Key activities in tracking the program's performance include:

- determining progress against the project plan,

- communicating to stakeholders the status of assigned activities,

- documenting significant deviations in performance, and

- taking corrective actions to address issues when necessary.[37]

Additionally, as we have previously reported, the implementation of IV&V is a best practice for large and complex system development and acquisition programs, and can provide important information to help

---

[37]CMMI-ACQ, Version 1.3 (November 2010).

program officials monitor and control their programs.[38] To be effective, IV&V activities should be performed by an entity that is independent of the management processes and products that are being reviewed.

CANES

The Navy had implemented the key project monitoring and control practices for CANES.

- **Determine progress against the project plan.** The program office regularly monitored progress of its prime contractor against the program schedule. For example, the program maintained an integrated master schedule and an integrated master plan to track progress against scheduled activities.

- **Communicate to stakeholders the status of assigned activities.** The program regularly communicated the status of assigned activities and work products to stakeholders. For instance, the program reported on its progress at weekly and monthly program office meetings that included, among others, the program manager, integrated product teams, contractor staff, and representatives from other program offices.

- **Document significant deviations in performance.** The program had reported significant deviations from its project planning parameters. For instance, in August 2012, the program reported to Congress an 11-month deviation from its schedule for the start of its production and deployment phase.

- **Take corrective actions to address issues.** CANES had taken corrective actions to address program issues. For example, in May 2012, the program updated its plan for installing the CANES system on ships after program officials determined that the schedule did not align with ship availability.

- **Utilize an IV&V agent.** The program used an IV&V agent to conduct operational testing to determine the viability of the system configuration. Program officials stated that they also planned to use

---

[38]GAO, *Homeland Security: U.S. Visitor and Immigrant Status Indicator Technology Program Planning and Execution Improvements Needed*, GAO-09-96 (Washington, D.C.: Dec. 12, 2008) and *Information Technology: Actions Needed to Fully Establish Program Management Capability for VA's Financial and Logistics Initiative*, GAO-10-40 (Washington, D.C.: Oct. 26, 2009).

an IV&V agent to conduct application integration testing in January 2013 and to conduct the initial operational test and evaluation scheduled for the fall of 2013.

As a result, CANES had established and utilized effective project monitoring and control practices, which should enable the program to maintain an understanding of the program's progress. Doing so should better position the program to take appropriate corrective actions when program performance deviates significantly from planned performance.

DEAMS

The Air Force had implemented selected practices for DEAMS's project monitoring and control, but its ability to monitor progress against the project plan was limited because the program had not developed an integrated master schedule that was consistent with scheduling best practices, and the program had not appropriately managed corrective actions to closure.

- **Determine progress against the project plan.** While DEAMS program officials were measuring progress against the program's integrated master schedule, the program's integrated master schedule was not reliable. Specifically, as we previously reported in October 2010, the program's integrated master schedule did not fully incorporate best practices, such as capturing all activities in the schedule.[39] While the program recently developed an updated integrated master schedule, the extent to which it followed scheduling best practices was unclear. We currently have another study underway that is assessing the reliability of this updated integrated master schedule.

- **Communicate to stakeholders the status of assigned activities.** The program regularly communicated the status of its assigned activities and work products to relevant stakeholders. For example, in June 2012, the program held a design review with key stakeholders, such as representatives from the DEAMS Financial Management Office; Office of the Under Secretary of Defense for Acquisition, Technology, and Logistics; and the Program Executive Office, to review the preliminary design of the system that would be fielded during releases 1 and 2.

---

[39]GAO-11-53.

- **Document significant deviations in performance.** The program took steps to document significant deviations in performance. For instance, in 2010, the program documented the significant schedule delays that DEAMS had experienced in a critical change report, because the program had not achieved a full deployment decision within 5 years of funds first being obligated in April 2005.

- **Take corrective actions to address issues.** DEAMS did not take appropriate corrective actions to address issues. Specifically, in 2010, an early operational assessment of the system conducted by the Air Force identified 350 must-fix deficiencies in DEAMS. As a result, the system had a significant number of defects that required substantial manual intervention to keep the system working as intended at the two test sites at which it had been deployed, and there was high user dissatisfaction with the system. In February 2012, we recommended that the Air Force ensure that future system deficiencies identified through independent assessments were resolved or mitigated prior to further deployment of the systems.[40] However, the program did not take appropriate corrective actions to address these issues. Although program officials stated that they had addressed all of these issues, the Air Force conducted a follow-up assessment from May to June 2012 and found 210 new and 15 repeat "must-fix" deficiencies from 2010. In September 2012, the program developed an action plan to address the deficiencies, and while the program had addressed 172 deficiencies, the remaining 53 "must-fix" deficiencies had not been resolved by the time the Deputy Chief Management Officer authorized the deployment of DEAMS to a third test site. According to program officials, despite not addressing all of the deficiencies, they deployed to the third test site in order to test certain functionality and validate that the 172 deficiencies had been corrected. However, as demonstrated by the deployment of the system to the first two test sites which contained a substantial number of defects, the system did not perform as planned and resulted in high user dissatisfaction with the system. Implementing our prior recommendation to resolve or mitigate system deficiencies prior to future deployments should help ensure that the deployed system performs as it was intended.

- **Utilize an IV&V agent.** The program had assigned an IV&V agent to assess topics of concern that were identified by the DEAMS program

---

[40]GAO-12-134.

office. For example, in 2012, an IV&V assessment was conducted on the system's configuration management and requirements management processes, and the IV&V contractor made several recommendations to improve these processes. As of August 2012, the program management office was taking steps to implement the recommendations.

Additionally, our prior work has stressed the importance of stable leadership during times of organizational transformation. We have reported that productivity often decreases during an organizational change (such as turnover in the program manager position) because attention can become concentrated on critical and immediate integration issues and diverted from longer-term mission issues.[41] However, DEAMS has not maintained consistent leadership in the program, which has compounded multiple problems—significant system deficiencies, outdated risk management processes, and taking almost 9 years to establish an acquisition program baseline. In particular, the program has had frequent turnover in the program manager position, with four different program managers in the past 4 years. Specifically, the tenures of DEAMS' last four program managers were: (1) April 2007 to May 2010, (2) May 2010 to May 2011, (3) May 2011 to May 2012, and (4) May 2012 to present (as of March 2013).

In commenting on a draft of this report, DOD stated that the Air Force supports tenure agreements for individuals in key leadership positions. In this regard, the department stated that the original program manager and his successor completed 3-year tenures. The department also offered an explanation as to why there had been such frequent turnover in the DEAMS program manager position—stating that the Air Force had, in one instance, used an interim manager until a new program manager could be assigned and, in another instance, had reassigned a program manager based on prevailing needs of the Air Force, prior to completion of his tenure. The department added that it expects the current DEAMS program manager to complete a 3-year term.

GCSS-Army

Similar to DEAMS, the Army had implemented best practices for GCSS-Army project monitoring and control, but the program's ability to monitor progress against the project plan was limited because it also had not

---

[41]GAO, *Results-Oriented Cultures: Implementation Steps to Assist Mergers and Organizational Transformation*, GAO-03-669 (Washington, D.C.: July 2003).

developed an integrated master schedule that was consistent with scheduling best practices, and it was not effectively using its IV&V function to properly monitor its program.

- **Determine progress against the project plan.** While GCSS-Army program officials were measuring progress against the program's integrated master schedule, we previously reported that the integrated master schedule was unreliable. Specifically, we reported in October 2010 that the schedule did not fully incorporate scheduling best practices and recommended that the Army conform with best practices to improve the schedule.[42] At the end of 2012, the program completed updating its integrated master schedule. In 2013, we plan to conduct a study to, among other things, determine the reliability of this updated schedule.

- **Communicate to stakeholders the status of assigned activities.** GCSS-Army regularly communicated status on assigned activities and work products to stakeholders. Specifically, the program held weekly and monthly meetings with various stakeholders to review GCSS-Army's progress and performance.

- **Document significant deviations in performance.** The program documented significant deviations from project plans. For example, GCSS-Army reported a 10-month delay in its schedule for achieving full deployment decision, originally planned for February 2012. The program achieved full deployment decision in December 2012.

- **Take corrective actions to address issues.** GCSS-Army took corrective actions to address its issues. For example, according to program officials, in the second quarter of fiscal year 2012, the program identified a configuration issue with the system and took steps to correct it; the issue was resolved in the fourth quarter of fiscal year 2012.

- **Utilize an IV&V agent.** Although GCSS-Army had implemented an IV&V function to assist with monitoring and controlling the program, it was not using this function effectively because the IV&V contractor was not independent. Specifically, the contract for IV&V services was issued by the program office and, as such, the contractor reported directly to the program office. Although copies of the IV&V reports were provided

---

[42]GAO-11-53.

to Army's Program Executive Office Enterprise Information Systems in addition to the program office,[43] the IV&V contractor was responsible for evaluating the performance of the same entity that awarded the contract. This introduced the potential risk that the contractor may not want to be overly critical in order to encourage the program office to continue to do business with it. Additionally, the IV&V contractor had been embedded within the program. Specifically, it was actively involved in identifying risks to the program, managing those risks, and managing risks identified by the system integrator—as opposed to acting as a third party to verify and validate risks that the program office and system integrator had identified and were managing. For example, the IV&V contract specifically stated that the contractor was to maintain, update, and manage the risk system that the program uses. In December 2012, in response to our concerns, GCSS-Army officials stated they plan to establish a new contract in early 2013 that will require the IV&V agent to report to DOD's Program Executive Office Enterprise Information Systems, rather than the program office. While this action is a step in the right direction, the program had not yet articulated the specific roles and responsibilities of the IV&V agent in acting as a third party that validates and verifies the risks that the program office and system integrator identify. Until the program specifies the roles and responsibilities of the IV&V agent to ensure that it maintains its independence from the risk management processes that it reviews, the program jeopardizes its chances of getting the intended value of an IV&V function, thus hindering its ability to fully monitor and control the program.

Conclusions

Three of the 14 selected programs stayed within their cost and schedule estimates and system performance targets, while 11 of the selected programs experienced cost increases, schedule slippages, and/or system performance problems. As such, these 11 programs were either costing more than planned, taking longer than planned to deliver, and/or had not performed as intended.

---

[43]GCSS-Army is one of the program offices included in the Army's Program Executive Office Enterprise Information Systems office, which is intended to enable information dominance by developing, acquiring, integrating, and deploying enterprisewide, network-centric information management and communications to meet the Army's current and future mission requirements.

While a number of best practices for risk management, project monitoring and control, and requirements management have been implemented for the CANES, DEAMS, and GCSS-Army programs, DEAMS and GCSS-Army lacked certain key practices that were essential to appropriately managing program risks and effectively acquiring the systems. Specifically, with regard to GCSS-Army, the program's lack of a risk management system that ensures the program has access to a comprehensive, up-to-date log of all current and relevant risks and associated mitigation plans reduces assurances that GCSS-Army has appropriately mitigated all program risks. Further, until the program specifies the roles and responsibilities of the IV&V agent to ensure that it maintains its independence from the risk management processes that it reviews, the program jeopardizes its chances of getting the intended value of an IV&V function, thus hindering its ability to fully monitor and control the program.

In addition, DOD (in commenting on our draft report) attributed frequent turnover in the DEAMS program manager position to the use of an interim program manager and to the reassignment of another program manager before completion of his tenure. The department stated, however, that the Air Force supports tenure agreements for individuals in key leadership positions. DOD's tenure agreement and its stated intent to have the current DEAMS program manager complete a 3-year term should help to ensure more continuous leadership and overcome past performance problems.

Recommendations for Executive Action

To better ensure that GCSS-Army implements effective risk management and project monitoring and control practices, we are recommending that the Secretary of Defense direct the Secretary of the Army to direct the GCSS-Army program office to take the following two actions:

- establish a comprehensive risk log that maintains an aggregation of all up-to-date risks and associated mitigation plans, and

- specify the roles and responsibilities of the IV&V agent to ensure that it acts as a third party that validates and verifies the risks and mitigation plans developed by the program office and system integrator.

Agency Comments and Our Evaluation

We received written comments on a draft of this report from DOD's Assistant Secretary of Defense (Acquisition). The comments are reprinted in appendix III.

In its comments, the department concurred with two of our three recommendations and partially concurred with one of our recommendations. Specifically, the department concurred with our recommendations that the GCSS-Army program establish a comprehensive risk log that maintains an aggregation of all up-to-date risks and associated mitigation plans, and that the program specify the roles and responsibilities of its IV&V agent to ensure that it acts as a third party that validates and verifies the risks and mitigation plans developed by the program office and system integrator.

The department partially concurred with our recommendation to examine the causes for the frequent turnover in the DEAMS program manager position, and take steps to address the causes to prevent such frequent turnover in the future. In its comments, DOD provided an explanation for the turnover—stating that the turnover had, in one instance, resulted from the use of an interim program manager until a new program manager could be assigned and, in another instance, from the reassignment of a program manager based on prevailing needs of the Air Force. The department added that the Air Force supports tenure agreements for individuals in key leadership positions, and that the original program manager and his successor completed 3-year tenures. The department said it expects the current DEAMS program manager to complete a 3-year term. Having the program manager serve out his tenure will be critical to helping ensure the success of DEAMS; as such, our decision to make this recommendation was based on the fact that program officials did not previously provide an explanation for the frequent turnover in this position. The department's explanation and its stated intent to have the current program manager in place for 3 years support our recommendation. Accordingly, we have revised our discussion of this matter, as appropriate, and we have removed the recommendation from the final report.

In addition, we received technical comments via e-mail from a program analyst in the Office of the Under Secretary of Defense for Acquisition, Technology and Logistics, which we have incorporated, as appropriate.

We are sending copies of this report to the appropriate congressional committees; the Secretary of Defense; and other interested parties. In addition, the report will be available at no charge on the GAO website at http://www.gao.gov.

Should you or your staff have any questions on information discussed in this report, please contact me at (202) 512-6304 or melvinv@gao.gov. Contact points for our Offices of Congressional Relations and Public Affairs may be found on the last page of this report. GAO staff who made major contributions to this report are listed in appendix IV.

Valerie C. Melvin
Director
Information Management
    and Technology Resources Issues

List of Addressees

The Honorable Carl Levin
Chairman
The Honorable James M. Inhofe
Ranking Member
Committee on Armed Services
United States Senate

The Honorable Thomas R. Carper
Chairman
The Honorable Tom Coburn
Ranking Member
Committee on Homeland Security and Governmental Affairs
United States Senate

The Honorable Dick Durbin
Chairman
The Honorable Thad Cochran
Ranking Member
Subcommittee on Defense
Committee on Appropriations
United States Senate

The Honorable John McCain
United States Senate

The Honorable Howard P. "Buck" McKeon
Chairman
The Honorable Adam Smith
Ranking Member
Committee on Armed Services
House of Representatives

The Honorable Darrell E. Issa
Chairman
The Honorable Elijah Cummings
Ranking Member
Committee on Oversight and Government Reform
House of Representatives

The Honorable C.W. Bill Young
Chairman
The Honorable Pete Visclosky
Ranking Member
Subcommittee on Defense
Committee on Appropriations
House of Representatives

Appendix I: Objectives, Scope, and Methodology

The National Defense Authorization Act for Fiscal Year 2012 mandated that GAO select and assess Department of Defense (DOD) major automated information system (MAIS) programs annually through March 2018.[1] This report is the first in our series of annual assessments. Our objectives were to (1) describe the extent to which selected MAIS programs have stayed within planned cost and schedule estimates and met performance targets, (2) assess selected MAIS programs' actions to manage risks, and (3) assess the extent to which selected MAIS programs used key information technology (IT) acquisition best practices.

To address the first objective, we established the following criteria for selecting a sample of the 48 DOD MAIS programs that were included in DOD's 2011 MAIS annual reports:

- at least 50 percent of the planned fiscal year 2011 budget was for new development;

- a program baseline had been established;

- the program had not been fully implemented or recently terminated;

- the majority of development work was not being developed using firm-fixed price contracts;

- at least one enterprise resource planning system was included in our review;[2]

- at least two programs from each of the Departments of the Air Force, Army, and Navy, and the Defense Information Systems Agency were included in our review; and

- the programs had the largest planned total life-cycle costs when factoring in the above criteria.[3]

---

[1]Pub. L. No. 112-81 § 1078 (2011).

[2]An enterprise resource planning system is an automated system using commercial off-the-shelf software consisting of multiple, integrated functional modules that perform a variety of business-related tasks, such as general ledger accounting, payroll, and supply chain management.

Relying on these criteria, we made an initial selection of 10 programs. Next, we selected 2 additional programs that had the largest planned total life-cycle costs and met all of the above criteria except that they were using firm fixed-price contracts. The criterion we used to select the final 2 programs was that they had to be without an acquisition program baseline (APB) for the longest periods of time.

The 14 selected programs were:

- the Air Force's

  - Defense Enterprise Accounting and Management System (DEAMS) Increment 1,

  - Expeditionary Combat Support System (ECSS) Increment 1,

  - Financial Information Resource System,

  - Information Transport Services Increment 1, and

  - Mission Planning Systems Increment 4;

- the Army's

  - Global Combat Support System – Army (GCSS-Army),

  - Global Command and Control System – Army Block 4, and

  - Tactical Mission Command;

- the Navy's

  - Common Aviation Command and Control System Increment 1,

  - Consolidated Afloat Networks and Enterprise Services (CANES),

  - Distributed Common Ground System – Navy Increment 1, and

---

[3]During the course of our review, the Air Force's Expeditionary Combat Support System (ECSS) Increment 1 program was terminated in December 2012.The number of MAIS programs dropped from 48 programs in 2011 to 42 in 2012, due to programs being fully deployed, reclassified, or terminated.

- Navy Enterprise Resource Planning; and

- the Defense Information Systems Agency's

  - Global Combat Support System – Joint Increment 7 and

  - Teleport Generation 3.

To address the first objective, we analyzed and compared each selected
program's first APB cost estimate to the latest life-cycle estimate to
determine the extent to which planned program costs had changed. Since
the Air Force's ECSS had not established an APB estimate, we compared
its initial life-cycle cost estimate to its latest cost estimate. Similarly, to
determine the extent to which these programs stayed within planned
schedule estimates, we compared each program's first APB schedule to
the latest schedule. We relied on the thresholds established by statute to
describe the amount of any deviation (i.e., significant or critical) that each
program's latest life-cycle cost and schedule estimates experienced from
the first APB.[4]

To determine whether the selected programs met their performance
targets, we compared program and system performance targets against
actual performance data in test reports and program management
briefings. We reviewed the results of operational assessments and
program evaluations conducted on the systems. We also reviewed
additional information on each program's cost, schedule, and
performance, including program documentation, such as DOD's MAIS
annual and quarterly reports; information from the Office of Management

---

[4]10 U.S.C. § 2445c(c), (d). With regard to schedule and cost deviations, a program is
considered to have undergone a "significant" change when it has (1) experienced a
schedule change that will cause a delay of more than 6 months but less than a year; (2)
estimated its life-cycle costs to have increased by at least 15 percent, but less than 25
percent, over the original estimate; or (3) experienced a significant, adverse change in the
expected performance of the system. A program is considered to have undergone a
"critical" change when it has (1) experienced a schedule change that will cause a delay of
1 year or more; (2) estimated its life-cycle costs to have increased by 25 percent or more
over the original estimate; (3) failed to achieve a full deployment decision within 5 years
after the milestone A decision for the program or, if there was no milestone A decision, the
date when the preferred alternative is selected for the program; or (4) experienced a
change in the expected performance of the system or major IT investment to be acquired
under the program that will undermine the ability of the system to perform the functions
anticipated.

and Budget's IT Dashboard;[5] DOD's fiscal year 2012 exhibit 300s;[6] APBs; monthly status briefings; system test reports; and our prior reports. We also interviewed program officials from each of the selected MAIS programs to obtain additional information on cost, schedule, and performance. We provided our assessments to the program management offices of each selected program for comment. We aggregated and summarized the results of these analyses across the programs, as well as developed individual profiles for each program (see appendix II).

To address the second and third objectives, we selected 3 of the 14 programs included in the first objective for an in-depth review. Specifically, we selected the 2 programs that had the highest planned total life-cycle costs—CANES and GCSS-Army—and 1 program that had been without a baseline for the longest period of time—DEAMS.

To address the second objective, we reviewed risk management documentation from the three selected programs and compared it to key risk management best practices identified in the Software Engineering Institute's Capability Maturity Model® Integration for Acquisition (CMMI-ACQ).[7] These key practices included:

- identifying risks, threats, and vulnerabilities that could negatively affect work efforts;

- evaluating and categorizing each identified risk using defined risk categories and parameters, such as likelihood and consequence, and determining each risk's relative priority;

- developing risk mitigation plans for selected risks to proactively reduce the potential impact of risk occurrence; and

---

[5]The Office of Management and Budget's IT Dashboard is a public website that provides detailed information on federal agencies' major IT investments, including assessments of actual performance against cost and schedule targets.

[6]An exhibit 300 is also called the Capital Asset Plan and Business Case. It is used to justify resource requests for major IT investments and is intended to enable an agency to demonstrate to its own management, as well as to the Office of Management and Budget, that a major project is well planned.

[7]Software Engineering Institute, *Capability Maturity Model® Integration for Acquisition* (CMMI-ACQ), Version 1.3 (November 2010).

- monitoring the status of each risk periodically and implement the risk mitigation plan, as appropriate.

Specifically, we analyzed program risk documentation, including monthly risk logs and reports, risk-level assignments, risk management plans, risk mitigation plans, and risk board meeting minutes. Additionally, we interviewed program officials to obtain additional information about their risks and risk management practices.

To address the third objective, we analyzed each selected program's IT acquisition documentation and compared it to certain key requirements management and project monitoring and control best practices—including CMMI-ACQ practices and independent verification and validation practices—to determine the extent to which the programs were implementing these practices.[8] In particular, the key requirements management best practices were:

- establish criteria for identifying appropriate requirements providers;

- establish objective criteria for the evaluation and acceptance of requirements;

- assess the impact of requirements on existing commitments;

- review project plans, activities, and work products to ensure that they are consistent with the defined requirements; and

- ensure traceability between the requirements and work products.

Additionally, the key project monitoring and control best practices were:

- determine progress against the project plan,

- communicate to stakeholders the status of assigned activities,

- document significant deviations in performance,

- take corrective actions to address issues when necessary, and

---

[8]CMMI-ACQ and GAO, *Information Technology: DHS Needs to Improve Its Independent Acquisition Reviews,* GAO-11-581 (Washington, D.C.: July 28, 2011).

- utilize an independent verification and validation agent.

Specifically, we analyzed program management plans, acquisition strategies, concepts of operations, development contracts, milestone and baseline review documentation, independent verification and validation reports, significant and critical change documentation, system requirements documentation, requirements management plans, requirements change requests, system test and defect reports, and technical performance measures. Further, we interviewed program officials to obtain additional information on each program's management processes in these key IT acquisition areas.

We conducted this performance audit from January 2012 to March 2013 in accordance with generally accepted government auditing standards. Those standards require that we plan and perform the audit to obtain sufficient, appropriate evidence to provide a reasonable basis for our findings and conclusions based on our audit objectives. We believe that the evidence obtained provides a reasonable basis for our findings and conclusions based on our audit objectives.

Appendix II: Profiles of Selected DOD MAIS Programs

This section contains profiles of the 14 selected MAIS programs. Each profile presents data on the program's purpose and status, its latest cost and schedule estimates compared to the first APB for cost and schedule, as well as system performance data, where available.

The first page of each two-page profile contains a description of the program's purpose and a figure that provides a comparison of the program's first APB schedule to the program's latest schedule.[1] The first page also provides (1) essential program details, such as the name of the prime contractor, as well as the total number of contractors—which includes the prime contractor, as well as any other contractors (and in some cases subcontractors) supporting the program; (2) program costs, comparing the program's latest life-cycle cost estimate (broken down into acquisition and operations and maintenance costs) to its first APB; (3) deployment details, such as the number of expected users and locations the system will be deployed to; and (4) a summary of the cost, schedule, and performance of each program, which is further discussed on the second page of the profile.

The second page of each two-page profile provides detailed information on each program's status, costs, schedule, and performance. In the status section, we discuss recent and upcoming milestones and events for each program. In the cost section, we identify the extent to which the program's life-cycle cost estimate has changed from its first APB, as well as the causes for any changes identified. In the schedule section, we discuss the extent to which the program's schedule has changed from its first APB, and the causes for any schedule changes identified. Finally, in the performance section, we identify the extent to which each program has met its established measures, as well as discuss the results of system performance tests.

---

[1]A program's first APB contains the original life-cycle cost estimate, schedule estimate, and performance parameters that were approved for that program by the milestone decision authority. The first APB is established after the program has assessed the viability of various technologies and refined user requirements to identify the most appropriate technology solution that demonstrates that it can meet users' needs.

Common Aviation Command and Control System (CAC2S) Increment 1

The Navy's CAC2S is intended to be a scalable and flexible command, control, and communications system of systems that can be deployed via humvees, helicopters, airplanes, amphibious ships, and landing craft within 24 hours of receiving a movement order, to effectively command, control, and coordinate aviation operations. It is intended to replace existing aviation command and control equipment from 12 legacy systems.

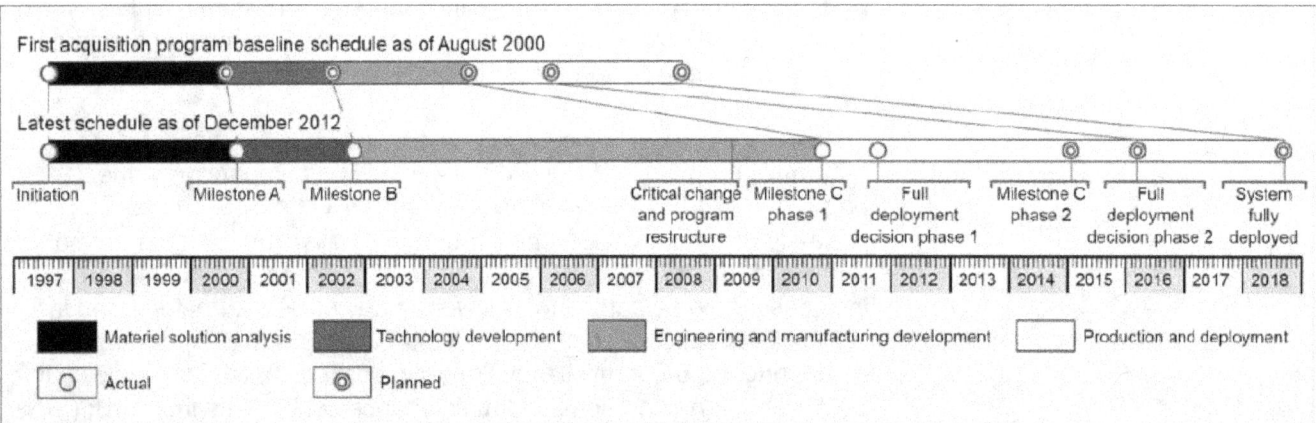

Source: GAO analysis of agency data.

Program Essentials (as of December 2012)

DOD component: Department of the Navy
Program owner: Program Executive Officer Land Systems (United States Marine Corps)

Prime contractor: General Dynamics
Total number of contractors: 5

Fiscal year 2013 funding requested: $84.1 million

Program Costs (then-year dollars in millions)

	First APB[a] (08/2000)	Latest Estimate[b] (09/2012)
Life-cycle cost estimate	$347.0	$2,352.9
Acquisition	173.4	869.8
Operations and maintenance	173.6	1,483.1
Amount spent to date (as of September 2012)	$453.2	

System Deployment Details (as of December 2012)

Current number of total expected users: 220 of 1592
Current number of total expected locations: 7 of 11

Legacy systems to be replaced: 12
Annual cost of legacy systems: $36.7 million

Number of system interfaces: 9

Cost, Schedule, and Performance Summary

» Exceeded planned cost estimate

» Exceeded planned schedule estimate

» Met system performance targets

Source: Data reported by DOD officials.

[a]The first APB estimate included the design, development, testing, and fielding of four systems to meet Tactical Air Operations Center requirements.

[b]The latest estimate included an increased program scope to design, develop, test, and field 70 systems to meet Tactical Air Operations Center, Direct Air Support Center, and Tactical Air Command Center requirements.

CAC2S Increment 1

Program Status

CAC2S Increment 1 is being developed and deployed in two phases. In October 2011, a full deployment decision was made to authorize CAC2S to begin fielding the first phase, which program officials stated consisted of 20 of CAC2S's 70 total systems. As of October 2012, program officials reported that these Phase 1 systems had been fielded to 7 of its 11 locations. In September 2012, the program awarded its development contract for Phase 2 (which is expected to consist of the remaining 50 systems) and plans to work on developing the system until January 2015. Initial operational testing for Phase 2 is scheduled for the third quarter of fiscal year 2015.

Exceeded Planned Cost Estimate

CAC2S experienced a critical cost estimate increase due to a large scope increase. Specifically, as of September 2012, CAC2S's life-cycle cost estimate was $2.35 billion, which was about a 578 percent increase from its first APB estimate, established in August 2000. Program officials attributed the increase in the cost estimate to the fact that the program's first APB estimate only included the design, development, testing, and fielding of four systems to meet Tactical Air Operations Center requirements. However, subsequent to establishing the first baseline, the program's scope was significantly increased to include Tactical Air Command Center and Direct Air Support Center requirements, as well as 66 additional systems. In March 2009, the program underwent a critical change and restructure. Subsequent to the program restructuring, program officials reported that CAC2S operated under budget in fiscal years 2011 and 2012.

Exceeded Planned Schedule Estimate

CAC2S experienced a critical schedule slippage, but met its rebaselined milestones. Program officials expect Increment 1 to be fully deployed in September 2018, about 10 years behind its first APB schedule. Several factors led to this delay. Specifically, in addition to the requirements added to the scope, as discussed above, the program determined that one of its contractors was unable to develop a solution that met the program's requirements. Program officials also determined that the program had insufficient contract controls (e.g., cost, schedule, and metrics) and risk controls in place and that the program office was understaffed. As a result, in March 2009, the program reported to Congress that it had experienced a critical schedule change and had restructured, as previously discussed. In November 2010, the program was rebaselined and, as of October 2012, had met its rebaselined milestones to date. In this regard, Phase 1 fielding was on schedule and the Phase 2 development contract had been awarded in September 2012, with fielding expected to commence in fiscal year 2016.

Met System Performance Targets

The 2011 initial operational testing and the 2012 limited user evaluations determined that Phase 1 was operationally effective and suitable. Additionally, in June 2012, the program office reported that CAC2S was meeting the targets for its two key performance metrics related to supporting DOD's integrated system architectures and displaying a common picture of real-time and non-real-time air operations data.

Consolidated Afloat Networks and Enterprise Services (CANES)

The CANES program was designed to consolidate and standardize the Navy's existing network infrastructures and services. This system is intended to, among other things, reduce and eliminate existing standalone afloat (i.e., surface ships and submarines) networks, provide a technology platform that can rapidly adjust to changing warfighting requirements, and reduce the hardware footprint on 259 afloat and maritime operations center platforms.

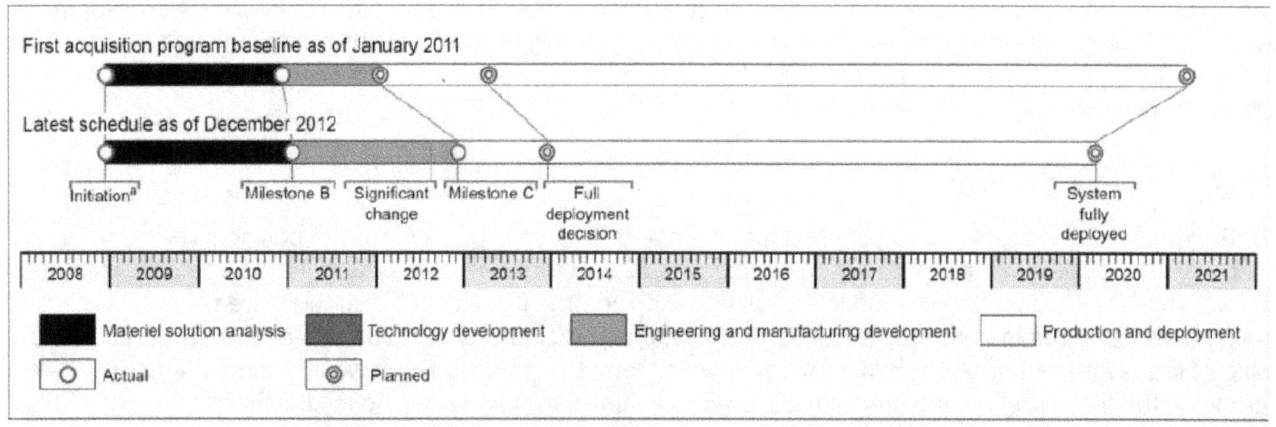

Source: GAO analysis of agency data.

[a]This date represents the funds first obligated date. According to program officials, milestone A was not required because the CANES program is a network consolidation, modernization, and integration effort that has no new technology development.

Program Essentials (as of December 2012)

DOD component: Department of the Navy
Program owner: Program Executive Office for Command, Control, Communications, Computers and Intelligence

Prime contractor: Northrop Grumman
Total number of contractors: 12

Fiscal year 2013 funding requested: $408.3 million

Program Costs (then-year dollars in millions)

	First APB (10/2010)	Latest Estimate (10/2012)
Life-cycle cost estimate	$12,740.9	$11,823.2
Acquisition	3,977.2	4,050.6
Operations and maintenance	8,763.7	7,772.6
Amount spent to date (as of September 2012)	$274.8	

System Deployment Details (as of December 2012)

Current number of total expected users: 0 of ~49,000
Current number of total expected locations: 0 of 259

Legacy systems to be replaced: 602
Annual cost of legacy systems: $14.2 million

Number of system interfaces: 6

Cost, Schedule, and Performance Summary

» Stayed within planned cost estimate

» Exceeded planned schedule estimate

» Did not fully meet system performance targets

Source: Data reported by DOD officials.

CANES

Program Status

In March 2010, the program began system development for CANES. The program completed operational testing in a lab environment in September 2012 and began its production and deployment phase with its first installation of CANES aboard a Fleet Destroyer in December 2012. Initial operational testing and evaluation performance tests are expected to be completed in October 2013. By December 2013, the Navy plans to decide on whether and how CANES will proceed into full production.

Stayed within Planned Cost Estimate

As of October 2012, the latest life-cycle cost estimate for CANES was approximately $11.8 billion, which represented about a 7 percent decrease from CANES's first APB cost estimate (approximately $12.7 billion). Program officials reported that the decrease was primarily a result of (1) the Navy's competition for the CANES prime contractor, which resulted in a lower than initially estimated cost for developing the CANES solution; and (2) the transfer of shipbuilding and conversion installation costs to other Navy programs. The officials projected that these actions will result in cost savings of $720.8 million (from fiscal years 2012 to 2018) and $166.2 million, respectively.

Exceeded Planned Schedule Estimate

CANES had accelerated its full deployment date, but experienced a recent delay in an interim milestone. As of December 2012, the program estimated that CANES would be fully deployed by 2020, which was a 1-year acceleration from the program's first APB estimate of 2021. Officials attributed the acceleration to reinvesting some of the cost savings from the procurement competition in order to increase the rate and number of installations aboard vessels. However, more recently, the planned start of the production and deployment phase was delayed by 11 months—from January 2012 to December 2012—which resulted in the program deferring network installations on three ships. Officials primarily attributed this delay to the fiscal year 2011 continuing resolution, which delayed the program by 6 months, and to a protest of the Navy's selection of the contractor for system development and demonstration, which delayed the program by approximately 1 month.

Did Not Fully Meet System Performance Targets

Performance tests that were conducted in a lab environment in July 2012 showed that 23 of 69 CANES requirements could not be fully demonstrated in the development model. These requirements were not fully met primarily due to the following reasons: (1) constraints of testing in the laboratory environment, which could not simulate certain conditions required on vessels, such as wireless connectivity, which was not available in the lab due to security concerns; (2) testing on a development model, which did not represent the final production model; (3) limited schedule—test period was 343 hours, but the reliability threshold is 495 hours; and (4) testing with only two hosted applications, while CANES is expected to host many applications. The remaining 46 CANES requirements were fully demonstrated in the development model.

Defense Enterprise Accounting and Management System (DEAMS) Increment 1

The DEAMS Increment 1 program is intended to provide 60 percent of the Air Force with the entire spectrum of financial management capabilities, including collections; commitments and obligations; cost accounting; general ledger; funds control; receipts and acceptance; accounts payable and disbursement; billing; and financial reporting. DEAMS is also intended to be a key component of the DOD plan for achieving fully auditable financial statements by September 30, 2017, as required by the National Defense Authorization Act for Fiscal Year 2010.[1]

[1]Pub. L. No. 111-84, § 1003(a) (2009) requires a plan that includes descriptions of actions and costs associated with ensuring that DOD financial statements are validated as ready for audit by not later than September 30, 2017.

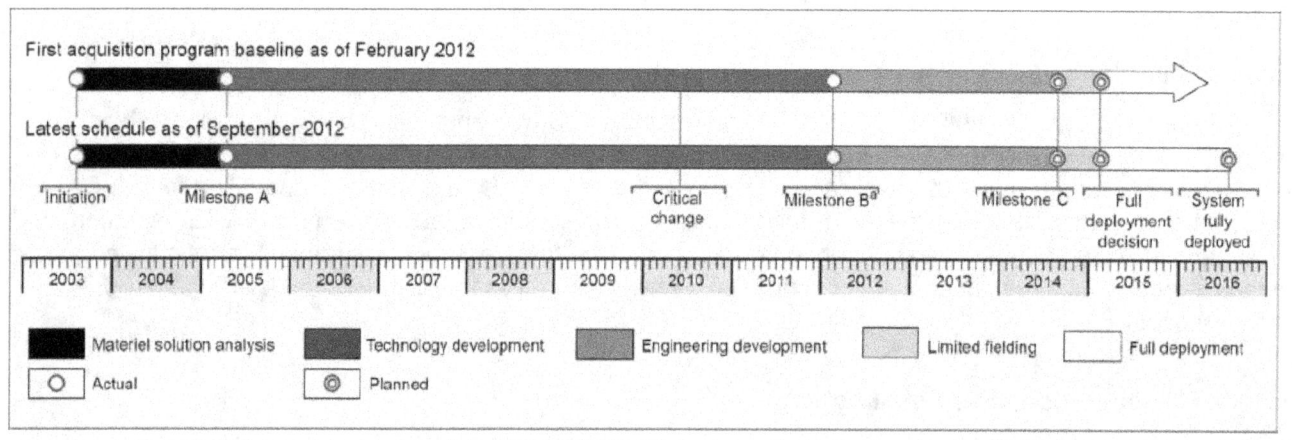

Source: GAO analysis of agency data.

[a]Prior to milestone B, the program was complying with the defense acquisition management system framework. Following milestone B in February 2012, the program began complying with the business capability life-cycle acquisition model. The program's revised acquisition strategy was also approved in February 2012.

Program Essentials (as of December 2012)

DOD component: Department of the Air Force
Program owner: Assistant Secretary for Financial Management and Comptroller

Prime contractor: Accenture
Total number of contractors: 24

Fiscal year 2013 funding requested: $119.5 million

Program Costs (then-year dollars in millions)

	First APB (02/2012)	Latest Estimate (09/2012)
Life-cycle cost estimate	$1,434.3	$1,434.3
Acquisition	853.2	853.2
Operations and maintenance	581.1	581.1
Amount spent to date (as of September 2012)	$369.9	

System Deployment Details (as of December 2012)

Current number of total expected users: at least 1,200 of 18,400
Current number of total expected locations: 3 of 76

Legacy systems to be replaced: 8
Annual cost of legacy systems: $56 million

Number of system interfaces: 84

Source: Data reported by DOD officials.

Cost, Schedule, and Performance Summary

» Stayed within planned cost estimate

» Stayed within planned schedule estimate

» Did not fully meet system performance targets

DEAMS Increment 1

Program Status

In July 2007 and May 2010, the Air Force began demonstrating certain DEAMS capabilities at two test locations: Scott Air Force Base and Defense Finance and Accounting Service Limestone, respectively. However, in May 2010, due to schedule delays (discussed below), the program underwent a critical change, which resulted in restructuring the development of DEAMS from two major releases to four. In February 2012, the program was restructured again to include six major releases that are to be deployed incrementally. Additionally, in February 2012, the program received approval to begin system development of release 1. In October 2012, it deployed release 1 to McConnell Air Force Base. The first release is scheduled to be fully deployed by the third quarter of fiscal year 2013.

Stayed within Planned Cost Estimate

As of September 2012, the program had not experienced a cost estimate increase since its first APB, which was established in February 2012. However, the program spent approximately $334 million and 9 years (see below) before establishing its first APB and developing a robust estimate for how much DEAMS was expected to ultimately cost.

Stayed within Planned Schedule Estimate

DEAMS had not experienced a schedule slippage since establishing its first APB, but it experienced a critical delay in establishing this APB. Specifically, the program was initiated in 2003 and the first APB was established in February 2012. Thus, the program had been underway for almost a decade before it developed a robust estimate for how long it was going to take to develop and implement DEAMS. Program officials attributed the delay, in part, to the complexity of reengineering business processes; evolving technical requirements; and designing, developing, and testing the software.

Did Not Fully Meet System Performance Targets

DEAMS had experienced many system performance defects and a majority of its performance measures needed attention or raised significant concerns. Specifically, in January 2011, Air Force's Test and Evaluation Center reported, among other things, that 350 must-fix deficiencies existed in the system. In August 2012, the Air Force's Test and Evaluation Center reported in its second operational assessment that 225 must-fix deficiencies existed in the system. Consequently, the Test and Evaluation Center recommended, among other things, that the program stabilize the system before proceeding further. In September 2012, program officials reported that they had resolved 172 of the 225 deficiencies, and as a result, the Deputy Chief Management Officer authorized DEAMS to be deployed at McConnell Air Force Base. Additionally, as of October 2012, for DEAMS's 38 performance metrics, the program had rated 15 green (i.e., normal), 11 yellow (i.e., needs attention), and 12 red (i.e., significant concerns).

Distributed Common Ground System – Navy (DCGS-N) Increment 1

DCGS-N Increment 1 is intended to provide integration of intelligence, surveillance, reconnaissance, and targeting support capabilities to the Navy's commanders on vessels and ashore to increase their battlespace awareness. It is intended to merge three existing Navy intelligence, surveillance, and reconnaissance systems into a single system. The program is being developed and deployed in two blocks—block 1 is intended to provide new hardware and software applications and decouple them from their existing computing environments, and block 2 is expected to move remaining applications to a new common computing environment for the Navy, which includes the CANES network.

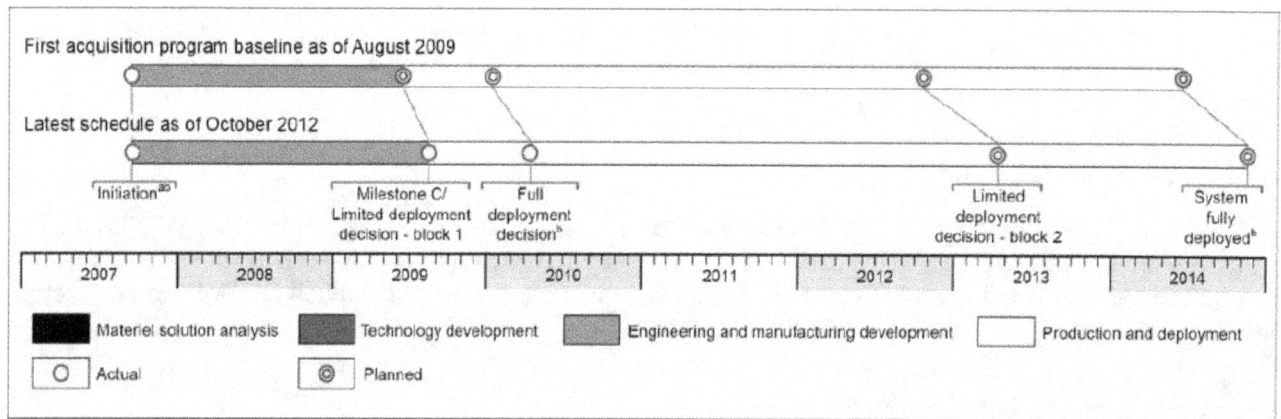

Source: GAO analysis of agency data.

[a]This date represents the funds first obligated date. The program entered the acquisition life-cycle at milestone C.

[b]This milestone includes the date provided in the updated baseline from April 2010. It was originally not specified in the first program baseline.

Program Essentials (as of December 2012)

DOD component: Department of the Navy
Program owner: Program Executive Office for Command, Control, Communications, Computers and Intelligence

Prime contractor: BAE Systems
Total number of contractors: 3

Fiscal year 2013 funding requested: $26.6 million

Program Costs (then-year dollars in millions)

	First APB (08/2009)	Latest Estimate (09/2012)
Life-cycle cost estimate	$1,434.3	$1,283.7
Acquisition	432.2	385.8
Operations and maintenance	1,002.1	897.9
Amount spent to date (as of September 2012)	$387.31	

System Deployment Details (as of December 2012)

Current number of total expected users: Unknown[a]
Current number of total expected locations: 20 of 34

Legacy systems to be replaced: 3
Annual cost of legacy systems: The cost of one legacy system is $2.2 million[b]

Number of system interfaces: 13

Cost, Schedule, and Performance Summary

» Stayed within planned cost estimate

» Exceeded planned schedule estimate

» Met system performance targets

Source: Data reported by DOD officials.

[a]Program officials did not provide the total population of possible users, but reported that the total number of expected workstations is 543.

[b]According to program officials, operations and sustainment costs of the remaining legacy systems were either not specified in program documentation or were not detailed enough to be provided.

DCGS-N Increment 1

Program Status

According to program officials, DCGS-N Increment 1, block 1 hardware and software is currently being deployed to certain vessels that have been designated as early adopters. As of December 2012, 20 block 1 systems were installed. In October 2012, the program initiated integration and testing efforts for block 2. Officials plan to reach a limited deployment decision for block 2 in April 2013 and operational testing for block 2 is scheduled for completion in October 2014.

Stayed within Planned Cost Estimate

As of September 2012, the latest life-cycle cost estimate was approximately $1.28 billion, which represented about a 10 percent decrease from the program's first APB estimate of $1.43 billion. Program officials reported that key factors contributing to the cost estimate decrease were a reduction in program funding; greater knowledge about block 2, which reduced certain program risks; and lower-than-expected costs associated with software development.

Exceeded Planned Schedule Estimate

As of October 2012, DCGS-N Increment 1's estimated full deployment date was November 2014, which represented a schedule slip of 5 months from the program's first APB schedule. Additionally, the estimated limited deployment decision for block 2 was delayed 6 months—from October 2012 to April 2013. Program officials reported that this delay was attributed to DCGS-N's block 2 dependency on the CANES network to operate—which had experienced delays (see CANES profile). Specifically, the fielding and testing plans for block 2 were closely tied to the deployment schedule for CANES. For example, according to program officials, the CANES network infrastructure needs to be available on a vessel before DCGS-N can begin the installation of block 2 applications on that vessel. The officials stated that, in April 2013, the program plans to decide if block 2 is ready to be deployed on a limited basis.

Met System Performance Targets

In December 2009, Navy reported after its initial operational test and evaluation that DCGS-N Increment 1, block 1 was operationally effective, operationally suitable, and ready for introduction into the Navy's fleet. The report noted that the system met or exceeded all of the expected performance metrics.

Expeditionary Combat Support System (ECSS) Increment 1

ECSS was intended to provide the Air Force with a single, integrated logistics system—including transportation, supply, maintenance and repair, engineering, and acquisition. ECSS was also intended to provide financial management and accounting functions. ECSS was to be a key component of the DOD plan for achieving fully-auditable financial statements by September 30, 2017, as required by the National Defense Authorization Act for Fiscal Year 2010. However, the program was canceled in December 2012.

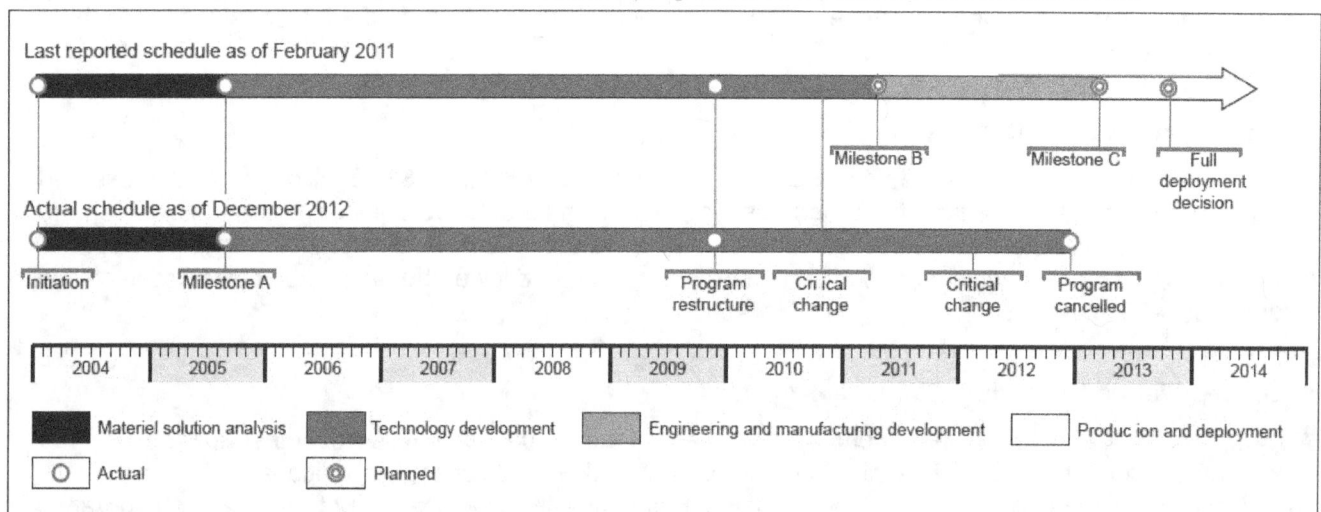

Source: GAO analysis of agency data.

Program Essentials (as of December 2012)

DOD component: Department of the Air Force
Program owner: Deputy Chief of Staff for Logistics, Installation, and Mission Support Headquarters

Prime contractor: Computer Sciences Corporation[a]
Total number of contractors: 12

Fiscal year 2013 funding requested: $187.9 million

Program Costs (then-year dollars in millions)

	Initial Estimate[b] (06/2005)	Last Estimate (02/2011)
Life-cycle cost estimate	$3,000	$3,197.3
Acquisition	1,800	2,270.5
Operations and maintenance	1,200	926.8
Amount spent to date (as of September 2012)	$1,029.1	

System Deployment Details (as of December 2012)

Current number of total expected users: 0 of 54,500
Current number of total expected locations: 0 of 225

Legacy systems that were to be replaced: 11
Annual cost of legacy systems: $79.8 million

Number of system interfaces: ~265

Cost, Schedule, and Performance Summary

» Exceeded planned cost estimate

» Exceeded planned schedule estimate

» Did not fully meet system performance targets

Source: Data reported by DOD officials.

[a]The contract with Computer Sciences Corporation was terminated in March 2012.

[b]The program, which was initiated about 9 years ago, never established an APB.

ECSS Increment 1

Program Status

In December 2012, DOD canceled the ECSS program due to numerous problems. Specifically, in early 2009, the Air Force determined that it had underestimated the size and complexity of ECSS and restructured the program into four increments, with the first to include three pilot efforts. In October 2010, ECSS increment 1 declared its first critical change because it had not reached a full deployment decision within 5 years from funds initially being obligated in August 2005. ECSS officials attributed this critical change to schedule delays (discussed below). After that critical change, increment 1 was restructured to include four pilots and the program increased the length of time for its system integrator to complete one of the initial pilots. In February 2012, the program underwent its second critical change because it had not established an APB and had not begun the engineering and manufacturing development phase in April 2011, as planned. Program officials attributed this to contractor performance issues (discussed in the performance section below). During the second critical change, the Air Force determined that ECCS was no longer a viable option for meeting the statutory requirement for financial auditability by 2017, since the scope of the program continued to decrease while costs increased and the schedule slipped.[1]

Exceeded Planned Cost Estimate

Prior to ECSS's cancelation, the program's cost estimate increased by 7 percent. As of February 2011, the reported life-cycle cost estimate was about $3.2 billion, which represented about a $200 million (approximately 7 percent) increase from the program's initial estimate of $3 billion. Program officials attributed the cost increase to schedule delays from the 2009 program restructure, two bid protests, and the refinement and addition of new requirements—such as financial and data requirements—into ECSS in 2008.

Exceeded Planned Schedule Estimate

ECSS experienced a critical schedule slippage. Specifically, prior to canceling the program, ECSS had experienced a 5-year slip in its planned date for achieving milestone B (authorizes a program to begin system development), which was initially scheduled for the fourth quarter of fiscal year 2007. Similar to the cost overruns, ECSS officials attributed the 5-year slip to the 2009 program restructure, two bid protests, and contactor performance issues (discussed below).

Did Not Fully Meet System Performance Targets

Poor system and contractor performance contributed to the cancelation of ECSS. Specifically, in April 2010, the Air Force's Test and Evaluation Center reported that the initial pilot had a limited scope, which impacted its ability to determine whether ECSS was on track to deliver desired performance. Additionally, the Test and Evaluation Center's interviews with subject matter experts and analysis of the limited data identified several system performance deficiencies, such as data quality issues. Moreover, program officials stated that, despite the extra time that the program office gave to the system integrator to fully develop and deploy one of the initial pilots, the system integrator was unable to complete the pilot. The contractor also was unable to meet the system performance requirements. As a result, in March 2012, the program terminated the system integrator's contract, and, as stated above, subsequently canceled the entire program.

---

[1]As of December 2012, the Air Force was in the process of developing a plan to modify its legacy systems in order to meet the 2017 financial auditability requirement. Air Force officials expected the plan to be completed by February 2013.

Financial Information Resource System (FIRST)

The Air Force's FIRST maintains an inventory of the department's force structure (i.e., organizations, weapons systems, and flying hours), and enables users to perform functions such as allocating aircraft vehicles and forecasting future aircraft attrition.

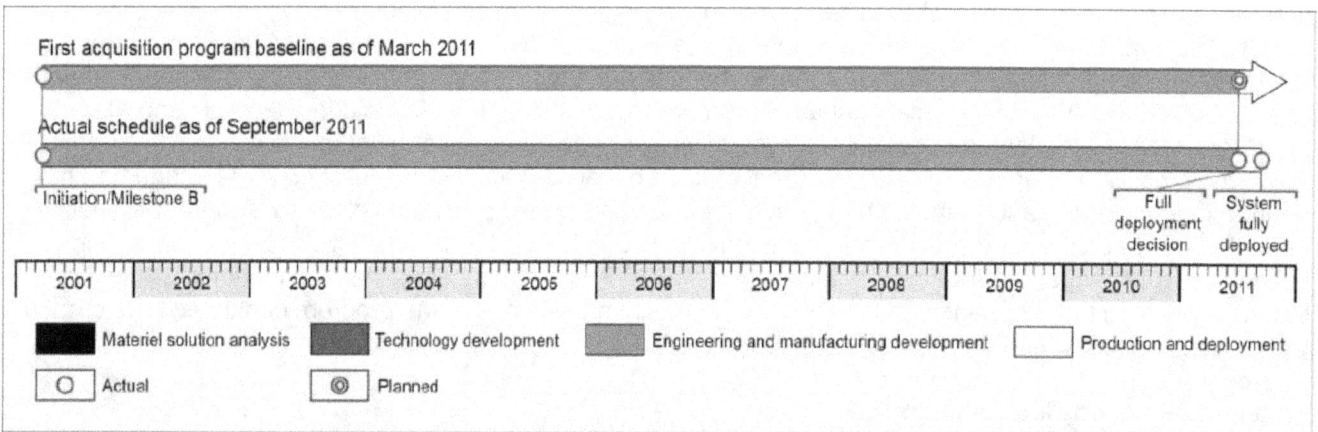

Source: GAO analysis of agency data.

Program Essentials (as of December 2012)

DOD component: Department of the Air Force
Program Owner: Financial Management and Comptroller

Prime contractors: Accenture Limited Liability Partnership and Lockheed Martin[a]
Total number of contractors: 3

Fiscal year 2013 funding requested: $700,000

Program Costs (then-year dollars in millions)

	First APB (03/2011)	Latest Estimate (09/2012)
Life-cycle cost estimate	$281.7	$227.0
Acquisition	181.8	167.5
Operations and maintenance	99.9	59.5
Amount spent to date (as of September 2012)	$180.77	

System Deployment Details (as of December 2012)

Current number of total expected users: 45 of 45
Current number of total expected locations: 2 of 2

Legacy system replaced: 1
Annual cost of legacy system: $450,000

Number of system interfaces: 3

Cost, Schedule, and Performance Summary

» Stayed within planned cost estimate

» Stayed within planned schedule estimate

» Met system performance targets

Source: Data reported by DOD officials.

[a]These were the primary contractors during software development. The system was fully developed and deployed by September 2011.

FIRST

Program Status

In September 2011, the Air Force completed its deployment of FIRST and the system is currently in an operations and maintenance status. However, while the program was initially intended to replace three legacy systems, in July 2010, the Air Force decided to replace only one legacy system—the Program Data System.[1] As a result, FIRST was not able to conduct budget formulation functions as originally intended. The system is currently scheduled to be retired in July 2013—less than 2 years after being fully deployed. DOD officials stated that the Air Force has decided to implement a new program that is intended to provide the remaining capabilities initially planned for FIRST.[2]

Stayed within Planned Cost Estimate

The program had experienced a cost estimate decrease due to reductions in scope and functionality. Specifically, as of September 2012, the latest life-cycle cost estimate (about $227 million) was about $54.7 million less than the program's first APB estimate of $281.7 million (about a 19 percent decrease). This decrease is primarily due to: (1) a decrease in the scope of the program's sustainment effort, since only one legacy system was replaced rather than the three that were originally planned (as discussed above); and (2) a reduction in the hardware required to maintain FIRST.

Stayed within Planned Schedule Estimate

The program did not experience schedule slippage against its first APB that was established in March 2011. Specifically, consistent with the program's first acquisition baseline schedule, full deployment decision occurred in July 2011.

Met System Performance Targets

In March 2011, an operational test and evaluation determined that the system was operationally effective and operationally suitable, but identified limitations in information assurance and interoperability. In August 2012, FIRST officials stated that these limitations were addressed prior to full deployment in September 2011.

---

[1]Program Data System was a legacy system that managed the department's force structure, flying hours, and attrition model capabilities.

[2]Program and Budget Enterprise Service is a software development effort intended to support the budget formulation and force programming process. Once deployed, this system is intended to result in the retirement of two legacy systems previously planned to be replaced by FIRST.

Global Combat Support System - Army (GCSS-Army)

GCSS-Army is intended to provide all active Army, National Guard, and Army Reserve tactical units worldwide with the capability to track supplies, spare parts, and organizational equipment. It is also to be used to track unit maintenance, total cost of ownership, and other financial transactions related to logistics for all Army units. Additionally, GCSS-Army is intended to be a key component of the DOD plan for achieving fully auditable financial statements by September 30, 2017, as required by the National Defense Authorization Act for Fiscal Year 2010. GCSS-Army is to be fielded in two waves—the first is to include releases 1.0 and 1.1 of the system, and is to provide warehouse and finance capabilities; and the second wave is to include release 1.2, which is to provide property book and maintenance capabilities.

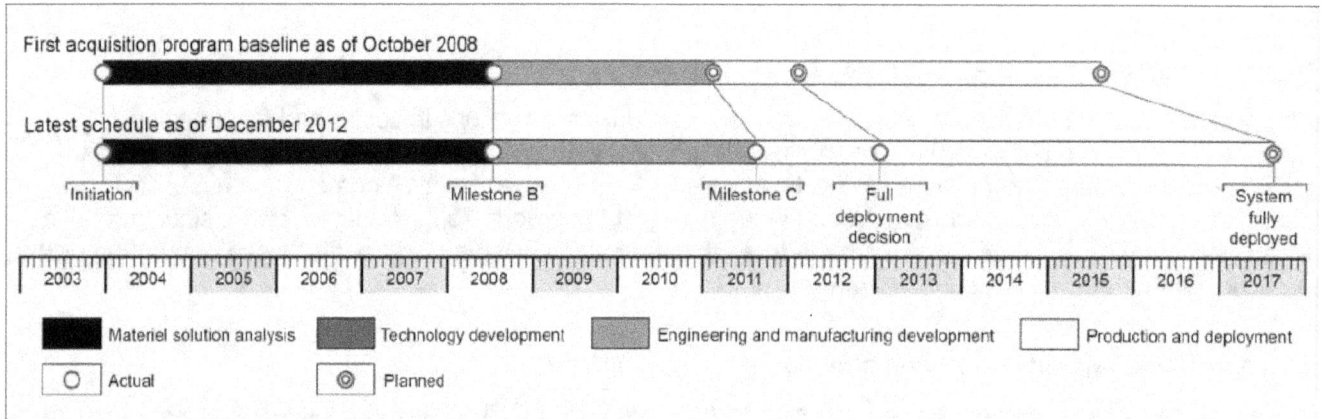

Source: GAO analysis of agency data.

Program Essentials (as of December 2012)

DOD component: Department of the Army
Program owner: Deputy Chief of Staff for Logistics, Army

Prime contractor: Northrop Grumman
Total number of contractors: 8

Fiscal year 2013 funding requested: $298.4 million

Program Costs (then-year dollars in millions)

	First APB (10/2008)	Latest Estimate (10/2012)
Life-cycle cost estimate	$3,968.9	$3,931.6
Acquisition	1831.9	1,955.8
Operations and maintenance	2,137.0	1,975.9
Amount spent to date (as of September 2012)	$1,138.1	

System Deployment Details (as of December 2012)

Current number of total expected users: 2,314 of 160,800
Current number of total expected locations: 7 of 379

Legacy systems to be replaced: 5
Annual cost of legacy systems: $92 million

Number of system interfaces: 127

Source: Data reported by DOD officials.

Cost, Schedule, and Performance Summary

» Stayed within planned cost estimate

» Exceeded planned schedule estimate

» Met system performance targets

GCSS-Army

Program Status

In December 2007, the program began testing release 1.0 of the GCSS-Army system with users at Fort Irwin, California. In August 2010, the program began conducting a limited user test of release 1.1 of the system at Fort Irwin. In August 2011, the program began operational testing of the system with users at Fort Irwin and at Fort Bliss, Texas. According to program officials, in November 2012, the program fielded release 1.1 of the system to five additional sites and continues to conduct validation testing at those sites. In December 2012, the program achieved full deployment decision, which allowed the program to deploy the system to all remaining locations.

Stayed within Planned Cost Estimate

As of October 2012, GCSS-Army's latest life-cycle cost estimate was about $3.93 billion, which was about a 1 percent decrease from its first APB estimate of approximately $3.97 billion—established in October 2008. Program officials attributed this decrease, in part, to renegotiating the cost of the contract for fielding the system.

Exceeded Planned Schedule Estimate

As of September 2012, GCSS-Army had experienced a 2-year slip in its full deployment date when compared to its first APB schedule—from the fourth quarter of fiscal year 2015 to the fourth quarter of fiscal year 2017. Officials attributed this delay to a change in the program's scope that was made to include both tactical and installation warehouses to support DOD's statutory requirement for auditability by fiscal year 2017. More recently, the program had experienced a 10-month slip in achieving the full deployment decision that was originally planned for February 2012. In November 2012, the program reported this significant delay to the congressional Armed Services and Appropriations Committees. In doing so, program officials attributed the delay to the discovery of configuration problems related to the scalability of the system, which resulted in the need for design corrections. Program officials reported that the corrections have since been implemented.

Met System Performance Targets

Based on limited testing of 545 users (less than 1 percent of the 160,800 planned users at full deployment), in June 2012, Army's Test and Evaluation Command reported that GCSS-Army release 1.1 was operationally effective, operationally suitable, and survivable against cyber threats. While it did not prevent the system from passing the evaluation test, the assessment report noted that the system did not reflect scaling for the projected number of users. According to program status documentation, during January 2012 through August 2012, the system's availability was 99.98 percent or greater each month.

Global Combat Support System – Joint (GCSS-J) Increment 7

The Defense Information Systems Agency's GCSS-J is a system that utilizes web-based technology to support military logistics operations by providing military personnel with the information about supplies that they need to accomplish their missions. The system combines data, such as the location of a particular resource (e.g., fuel), from multiple systems and analyzes the data to provide information needed by logistics decision makers at the Combatant Commands to ensure the right personnel, equipment, supplies, and support are in the right place at the right time and in the correct quantities.

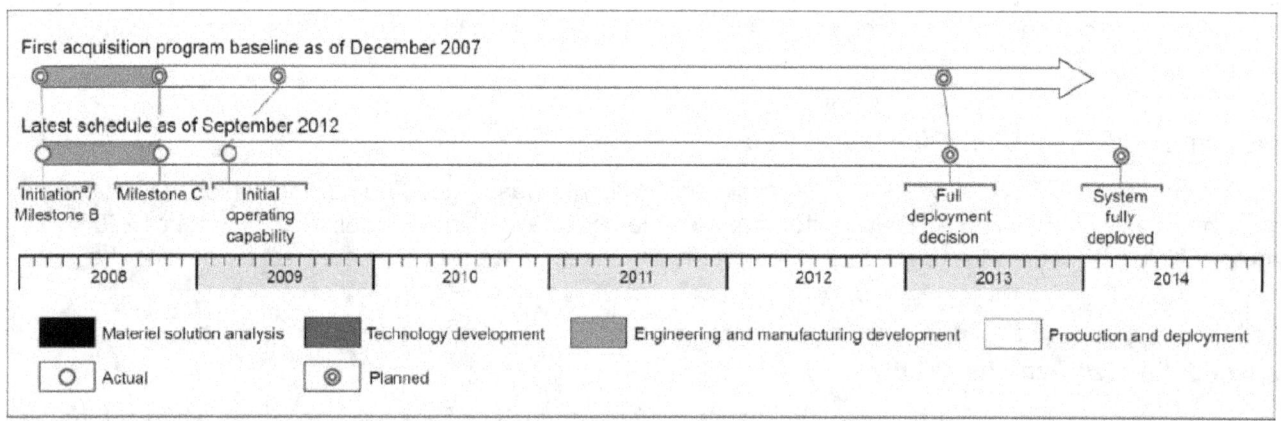

Source: GAO analysis of agency data

[a]According to program officials, the overall GCSS-J program was approved in September 1995 and Increment 7 was initiated at milestone B.

Program Essentials (as of December 2012)

DOD component: Defense Information Systems Agency
Program owner: Joint Staff J4 (Logistics)

Prime contractor: Northrop Grumman
Total number of contractors: 6

Fiscal year 2013 funding requested: $36.8 million

Program Costs (then-year dollars in millions)

	First APB (12/2007)	Latest Estimate (09/2012)
Life-cycle cost estimate	$209.6	$173.4
Acquisition	148.4	125.4
Operations and maintenance	61.2	48.0
Amount spent to date (as of September 2012)	$127.6	

System Deployment Details (as of December 2012)

Current number of total expected users: 134 of 999 (or less)
Current number of total expected locations: 7 of 7

Legacy systems to be replaced: 0
Annual cost of legacy systems: $0

Number of system interfaces: 25

Cost, Schedule, and Performance Summary

» Stayed within planned cost estimate

» Stayed within planned schedule estimate

» Met system performance targets

Source: Data reported by DOD officials.

GCSS-J Increment 7

Program Status

In October 2008, GCSS-J Increment 7 entered the production and deployment phase. Since April 2010, the program has been developing and deploying increments of functionality (referred to as releases) approximately every 6 months. Its latest release (7.3.2) was deployed in October 2012, and provided capabilities such as the ability to view worldwide munitions inventory and trend charts for fuel levels. The program is currently developing capabilities for its final major release (7.4), which is intended to refresh the system infrastructure and enable users to customize their web-based view of various logistics data sources, thus allowing users more flexibility to display only the information relevant to their mission. Currently, GCSS-J is operating at seven Combatant Command locations.

Stayed within Planned Cost Estimate

As of September 2012, the latest life-cycle cost estimate was approximately $173.4 million, which is about a 17 percent decrease from GCSS-J Increment 7's first APB estimate of $209.6 million—established in December 2007. Program officials attribute the decrease to budget cuts that have reduced the number of engineering hours available to develop system capabilities. The officials stated that the total scope of the program has not changed because the program's incremental development approach allowed the requirements to be reprioritized and developed based on available funding.

Stayed within Planned Schedule Estimate

As of September 2012, GCSS-J officials reported that it was on track to achieve Increment 7's full deployment decision in March 2013, as planned. In addition, the program expects to reach full deployment in March 2014.

Met System Performance Targets

The program office reported that, as of March 2012, GCSS-J Increment 7 (through release 7.3.1) had fully met five of six key performance metrics, including system availability and responsiveness to asset data queries. The system had partially met its metric regarding responsiveness of joint decision support tools. According to program officials, full compliance with this metric was deemed inappropriate until GCSS-J and its counterpart GCSS systems within other military branches have achieved full operational capability.[1] In addition to its key performance metrics, program officials stated that user satisfaction with Increment 7 has improved since release 7.2. For example, most users were reported to be satisfied with the system's mapping capability, which allows users to visualize where commodities are located and determine their status.

---

[1]Other GCSS systems include GCSS-Army and GCSS-Marine Corps.

Global Command and Control System – Army (GCCS-A) Block 4

The Army's GCCS-A Block 4 includes hardware and software products that are to provide command and control capabilities that support the Army and Joint Commander's need for a fused, real-time, true picture of the battlespace and the ability to command, control, and coordinate the information necessary to accomplish a mission within the battlespace. GCCS-A is to interface with various DOD systems to share operational information and data between strategic commanders and staff in combat areas.

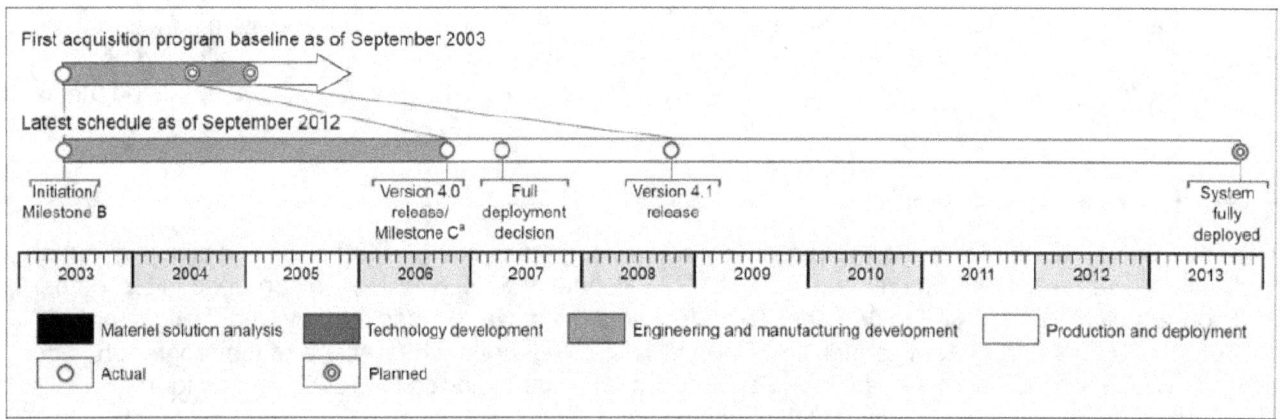

Source: GAO analysis of agency data.

[a]Milestone C was not included in the first APB schedule. The release of version 4.0 was included in both the first APB schedule and the latest schedule.

Program Essentials (as of December 2012)

DOD component: Department of the Army
Program owner: Army's Strategic Mission Command

Prime contractor: Lockheed Martin
Total number of contractors: 19

Fiscal year 2013 funding requested: $25.4 million

Program Costs (then-year dollars in millions)

	First APB (09/2003)	Latest Estimate (09/2012)
Life-cycle cost estimate	$837.8	$474.9
Acquisition	462.5	365.5
Operations and maintenance	375.3	109.4
Amount spent to date (as of September 2012)	$353.9	

System Deployment Details (as of December 2012)

Current number of total expected users: Unknown[a]
Current number of total expected locations: 91 of 116

Legacy systems to be replaced: 0
Annual cost of legacy systems: $0

Number of system interfaces: 36

Cost, Schedule, and Performance Summary

» Stayed within planned cost estimate

» Exceeded planned schedule estimate

» Met system performance targets

Source: Data reported by DOD officials.

[a]The program only tracks the number of hardware procurements, not the number of users.

GCCS-A Block 4

Program Status

In October 2006, GCCS-A Block 4 released version 4.0—the first of four planned software releases. In October 2008, the program began fielding the second release—4.1. The Army decided not to pursue the final two releases and to instead replace GCCS-A with a new DOD-wide command and control system, called Net-Enabled Command Capability. However, in November 2009, Net-Enabled Command Capability was canceled due to challenges experienced in developing and managing requirements from the different military branches. Thus, the Army now plans to deliver the remaining desired functionally in another program. Currently, GCCS-A is maintaining version 4.1 and developing software patches, as necessary, as well as continuing to field GCCS-A hardware to users worldwide. Program officials expected to have Block 4 fully deployed by October 2013.

Stayed within Planned Cost Estimate

As of September 2012, the latest life-cycle cost estimate for GCCS-A was $474.9 million, which is a 43 percent decrease from the program's first APB estimate of $837.8 million. This decrease was primarily due to a reduction in the planned operations and maintenance costs, which program officials attributed, in part, to evolving technology changes that enabled the program to use a virtual operations and maintenance environment.

Exceeded Planned Schedule Estimate

GCCS-A had experienced a significant 3-year slippage in its full deployment date compared to its first complete APB schedule. Specifically, program officials planned to fully deploy the system by October 2010; however, as of September 2012, the program estimated that the system would be fully deployed in October 2013. The project manager reported that this slip was due, in part, to the cancellation of Net-Enabled Command Capability, which required the Army to continue fielding GCCS-A beyond the originally identified units and continue maintaining version 4.1 longer than originally planned. Additionally, GCCS-A experienced over a 2-year slip in the release of version 4.0 and a nearly 4-year slip in the release of version 4.1, which program officials attributed to adhering to new Army requirements mandating that it align its schedule to other DOD command and control systems to ensure interoperability.

Met System Performance Targets

GCCS-A was meeting its system performance measures. In this regard, an Army facility tested the GCCS-A system in July 2011 and determined that it was performing as intended. Specifically, the system met its performance measures in areas such as system interoperability and information assurance compliance requirements.

Information Transport Services (ITS) - Increment 1[1]

The Air Force's ITS Increment 1 program is intended to provide the core network infrastructure, such as network cables and servers, for over 150 active duty, Air Force Reserve, and Air National Guard bases. Specifically, the program is to update the fixed local area network and all necessary information transport infrastructure in order to support current and future communications needs of the Air Force and Joint Command warfighter. Prior to becoming a standalone MAIS program, these capabilities were originally planned to be provided by the Combat Information Transport System program, but in April 2009, this program was restructured into two smaller programs—ITS and Air Force Intranet.[2]

[1]In December 2012, program officials stated that the program's name was changed to Base Information Transport Infrastructure.

[2]The Combat Information Transport System program portfolio was intended to provide the information infrastructure, network management, and network defense capabilities to meet the multimedia information transport needs of Air Force bases.

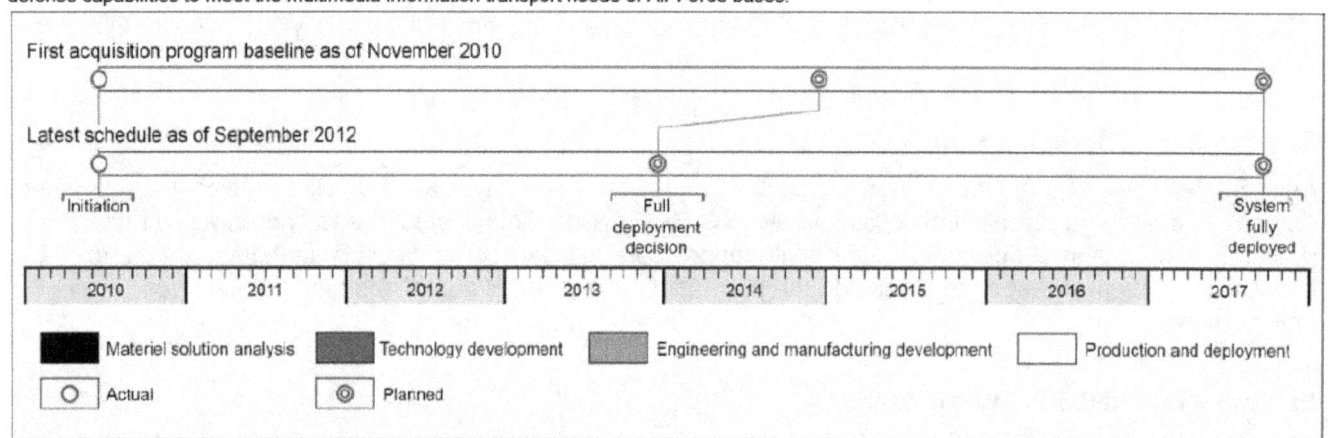

Source: GAO analysis of agency data.

Program Essentials (as of December 2012)

DOD component: Department of the Air Force
Program owner: Commander, Air Force Space Command

Prime contractor: Varies by installation[a]
Total number of contractors: 9

Fiscal year 2013 funding requested: $32.5 million

Program Costs (then-year dollars in millions)

	First APB (11/2010)	Latest Estimate (11/2012)
Life-cycle cost estimate	3,789.9	$3,399.5
Acquisition	1,417.7	1,254.6
Operations and maintenance	2,372.2	2,144.9
Amount spent to date (as of November 2012)	$1,100	

System Deployment Details (as of March 2013)

Current number of total expected users: 1,061,568 of 1,239,132
Current number of total expected locations: 139 of 178

Legacy systems to be replaced: not applicable[b]
Annual cost of legacy systems: not applicable[b]

Number of system interfaces: not applicable[b]

Cost, Schedule, and Performance Summary

» Stayed within planned cost estimate

» Stayed within planned schedule estimate

» Met system performance targets

Source: Data reported by DOD officials.

[a]The program uses a multiple award contract that includes several contractors. For each installation, one contractor is selected to complete the infrastructure upgrades at that installation.
[b]This is a hardware replacement effort. Future installations have not yet been surveyed.

ITS Increment 1

Program Status

In June 2010, funds were first obligated to ITS Increment 1. As of March 2013, program officials reported that the infrastructure upgrades had been completed at 139 of the 178 locations planned for Increment 1. The program was working on upgrading the infrastructure at 39 remaining locations. In December 2012, program officials stated that the program name had been changed to Base Information Transport Infrastructure.

Stayed within Planned Cost Estimate

As of November 2012, the latest life-cycle cost estimate for ITS Increment 1 was approximately $3.4 billion, which was about a 10 percent decrease from the program's first APB estimate of about $3.8 billion in November 2010. ITS officials stated that the decrease in program costs was mainly due to contractors submitting proposals for the infrastructure upgrades at each installation that were approximately 40 percent lower than what the program office expected based on past proposals. However, in March 2013, program officials reported that hardware refresh cycles are projected to extend from 6 years to 10 years based on the current fiscal year 2013 funding levels. This is expected to result in increased sustainment costs for end-of-life equipment that will need to be maintained longer. ITS officials stated that they plan to work with Air Force officials to try to restore funding to the 6-year refresh cycle.

Stayed within Planned Schedule Estimate

As of November 2012, ITS Increment 1 had not experienced schedule slippages and ITS officials stated that they were on track to meet the September 2017 full deployment date. This date is consistent with the full deployment date identified in the program's first APB estimate. In September 2012, the Office of the Secretary of Defense reported that current funding levels may affect the program's ability to meet the September 2017 full deployment date. To mitigate this funding issue, program officials stated that the program office has changed its funding strategy to allow infrastructure upgrades to be completed using funding from 2 fiscal years, rather than 1.

Met System Performance Targets

As of September 2012, the program was meeting all four of its performance measures related to interoperability, availability, support, and reliability. For example, data transfer tests and router redundancy tests were performed and passed at locations prior to government acceptance.

Mission Planning Systems (MPS) Increment 4

The Air Force's MPS Increment 4 program is a collection of individual programs that is intended to provide flight and weapons delivery planning. MPS Increment 4 is to migrate legacy mission planning aircraft capabilities to a collaborative, single multiservice system. This system is intended to support the development of detailed flight plans and improve effectiveness by enabling the exchange of threat, target, terrain, weather, and aircraft performance capability information between warfighters, aircrews, and operational planners.

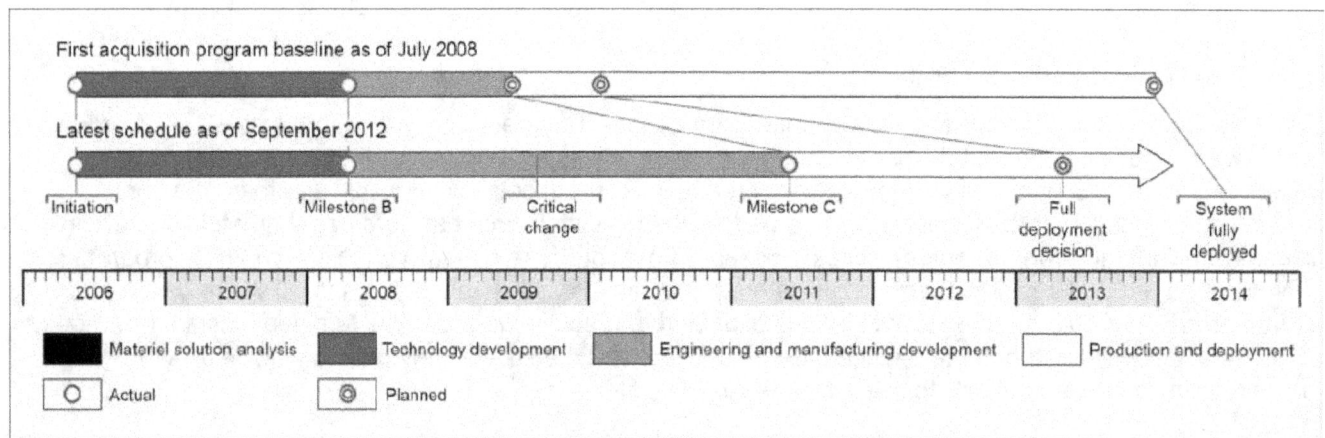

Source: GAO analysis of agency data.

Program Essentials (as of December 2012)

DOD component: Department of the Air Force
Program owner: Air Combat Command

Prime contractor: not applicable[a]
Total number of contractors: 29

Fiscal year 2013 funding requested: $7.9 million

Program Costs (then-year dollars in millions)

	First APB (07/2008)	Latest Estimate (09/2012)
Life-cycle cost estimate	$639.9	$303.8
Acquisition	326.5	252.1
Operations and maintenance	313.4	51.7
Amount spent to date (as of September 2012)	$242	

System Deployment Details (as of December 2012)

Current number of total expected users: 2,975 of 3,580
Current number of total expected locations: 87 of 100

Legacy system to be replaced: 1
Annual cost of legacy system: $12.5 million

Number of system interfaces: 26

Cost, Schedule, and Performance Summary

» Stayed within planned cost estimate

» Exceeded planned schedule estimate

» Did not fully meet system performance targets

Source: Data reported by DOD officials.

[a]The government has taken on the responsibility of managing each of the contractors that support the MPS program.

MPS Increment 4

Program Status

In September 2009, due to schedule delays and other funding priorities (discussed below), MPS Increment 4 was restructured and 9 of 18 planned developments and upgrades to aircraft were canceled. The program also changed from replacing three legacy systems, as originally planned, to replacing one legacy system. In February 2012, another planned development was canceled because of cuts to the program's fiscal year 2013 budget. As a result, the program's scope was reduced to modernizing the mission planning capabilities on a total of eight aircraft. As of November 2012, the mission planning capabilities for six of the aircraft had been deployed and the capabilities for one of the aircraft were being tested. The design and development of the capabilities for the eighth aircraft are not expected to be complete until fiscal year 2014.

Stayed within Planned Cost Estimate

The planned life-cycle cost estimate for MPS Increment 4 had decreased due to scope and functionality reductions. Specifically, as of September 2012, the latest life-cycle cost estimate (about $303.8 million) was approximately 53 percent less than the program's first APB cost estimate (about $639.9 million). Program officials reported that the decrease in costs was due to the termination of the planned development and upgrade activities for 10 of the 18 aircraft originally included in Increment 4, and a lower estimate for operations and maintenance costs because of this reduced scope.[1]

Exceeded Planned Schedule Estimate

The program has experienced about a 3-year critical schedule slip in the planned date for full deployment decision. Program officials reported that schedule delays were due, in part, to the complexity of developing, integrating, and testing mission planning capabilities, and incorporating unplanned development work in order to integrate with the Air Force's new operating system. The program also experienced schedule delays due to additional time needed to address system performance problems (discussed in detail below). The full deployment date for MPS Increment 4 had not yet been determined; program officials expected it to be established at the program's full deployment decision review, currently scheduled for May 2013.

Did Not Fully Meet System Performance Targets

In 2011, operational testing identified significant deficiencies with MPS Increment 4 capabilities for one of the aircraft. The program has since developed patches to address many of the deficiencies. In November 2012, program officials stated that the Air Force's Test and Evaluation Center was conducting operational tests to determine whether the previously identified deficiencies had been corrected; however, as of December 2012, the results of these tests were not known. Operational tests that have been conducted on the mission capabilities for six other aircraft determined that these aircraft were operationally effective and suitable.

---

[1]Program officials also stated that certain capabilities that were terminated from MPS are now expected to be delivered in two other Air Force modernization programs that were initiated in April 2012—Air Mobility Command Transition and Mobility Air Forces Automated Flight Planning Service.

Navy Enterprise Resource Planning (ERP)

Navy ERP is intended to replace segregated legacy systems with a single integrated software system that provides an end-to-end supply chain solution for receiving, processing, and fulfilling requests for resources; integrated financial management; workforce management; inventory management; material operations; and rapid response to logistical needs of operating forces.

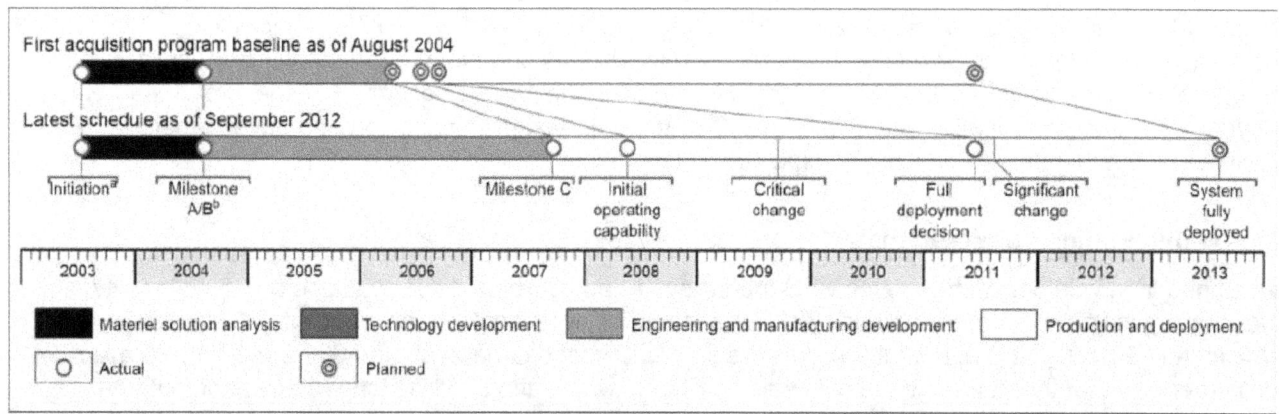

Source: GAO analysis of agency data.

[a]According to program officials, the Navy ERP initiation date was August 2004, and the July 2003 initiation date reported in GAO-11-53 represented the date that the Navy ERP program received its acquisition category designation.

[b]According to program officials, the Navy ERP program was created on the convergence of four pilot programs, which resulted in accomplishing milestones A and B on the same date.

Program Essentials (as of December 2012)

DOD component: Department of the Navy
Program owner: Chief of Naval Operations

Prime contractors: IBM, Deloitte, iLuMina Solutions, Herren Associates
Total number of contractors: 28

Fiscal year 2013 funding requested: $136.4 million

Program Costs (then-year dollars in millions)

	First APB (08/2004)	Latest Estimate (09/2012)
Life-cycle cost estimate	$1,992.7	$2,601.5
Acquisition	679.2	1,046.4
Operations and maintenance	1,313.5	1,555.1
Amount spent to date (as of September 2012)	$1,449.0	

System Deployment Details (as of December 2012)

Current number of total expected users: ~72,000 of ~72,000
Current number of total expected locations: 108 of 108

Legacy systems to be replaced: 89
Annual cost of legacy systems: $103 million

Number of system interfaces: 48

Source: Data reported by DOD officials.

Cost, Schedule, and Performance Summary

» Exceeded planned cost estimate

» Exceeded planned schedule estimate

» Did not fully meet system performance targets

Navy ERP

Program Status

As of November 2012, program officials reported that Navy ERP had been fielded to all 108 locations and 72,000 users. Its most recent deployments occurred in October 2012 to the Office of Naval Research and Strategic Systems Program. While the system has been fully fielded, the program has been working to stabilize the system (see performance discussion below) in order to achieve full deployment, planned for August 2013. Towards that end, officials stated that they were planning to begin the final operational test and evaluation of the supply solution management functionality in January 2013.

Exceeded Planned Cost Estimate

As of September 2012, the life-cycle cost estimate for the program was approximately $2.6 billion, which represented a cost increase of 31 percent from its first APB cost estimate of about $2.0 billion. In this regard, the program reported to Congress in August 2011 that it had experienced a significant change in its life-cycle cost estimate. Program officials attributed the life-cycle cost increases to schedule slippages, an increase in demand for on-site support and stabilization activities during system deployments, and adding requirements to support business process reengineering and improved financial management information.

Exceeded Planned Schedule Slippage

Navy ERP is expected to be fully deployed in August 2013—more than 2 years behind its first APB estimate of June 2011. This delay is the result of several changes in the program, such as a September 2009 critical change to remove certain maintenance requirements from the program. Additionally, in August 2011, the program underwent a significant change in its schedule due to the identification of a substantial number of system deficiencies during supply solution initial testing, and, as a result, the program failed to achieve its full deployment decision in September 2010, as planned. Full deployment decision was later achieved in June 2011. Program officials also attributed the delay to changes that were implemented based on lessons learned from an earlier deployment, including adding data conversion resources because the cleansing of legacy data required more effort than anticipated; and adding additional time for each deployment to reduce risk and fully support transitions. Additionally, final operational testing and evaluation were delayed from April 2012 to January 2013 due to the need for additional time to mitigate system deficiencies (see below).

Did Not Fully Meet System Performance Targets

Navy ERP had partially met its system performance measures and substantial system deficiencies remained. Specifically, as of September 2012, program officials reported Navy ERP was meeting one of its two key performance metrics. In December 2012, program officials reported that the performance measure that it did not meet (related to processing time) may not be related to the Navy ERP system and that root causes would be further identified during the final operational testing and evaluation scheduled to begin in January 2013. In addition, while the program had been working to address a significant number of system deficiencies that were identified in September 2010, officials reported as of December 2012 that 560 system defects remained open. The officials stated that they continued to address those deficiencies and that the critical mission performance deficiencies were scheduled for mitigation by the second quarter of fiscal year 2013.

Tactical Mission Command (TMC)

TMC is a suite of products—including both hardware and software—that are intended to provide Army and joint community commanders and their staffs with improved battle command capabilities, such as real-time situational awareness and displays of unified information on subject matters, such as friendly forces and enemy forces (referred to as the common operational picture). TMC products have been fielded worldwide and are intended to support decisionmaking, planning, rehearsal, and execution management. One key component—known as Command Post of the Future—is to provide an executive-level decision support capability with real-time collaboration tools.

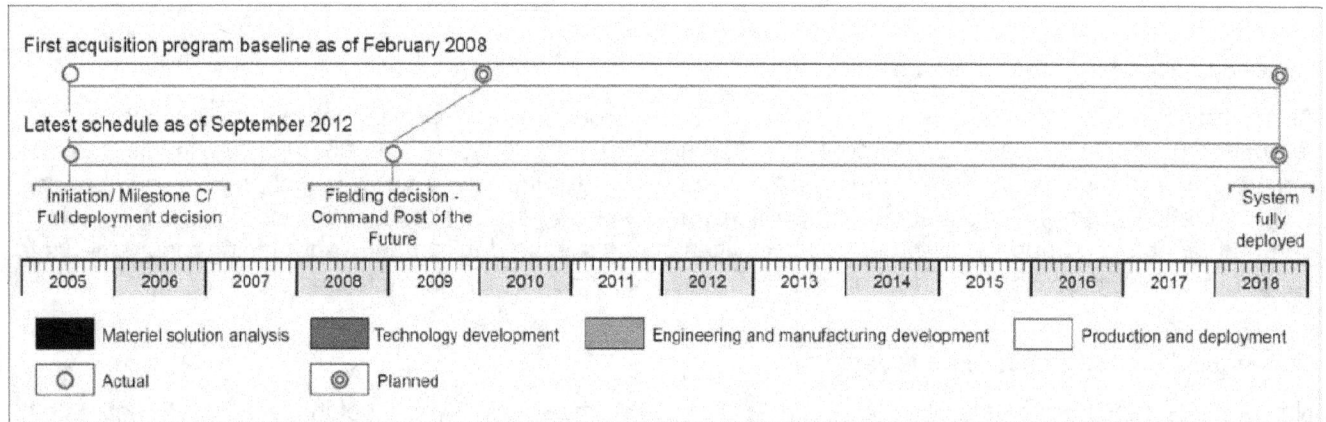

Source: GAO analysis of agency data.

Program Essentials (as of December 2012)

DOD component: Department of the Army
Program owner: Project Manager Mission Command, Program Executive Office Command, Control, and Communications-Tactical

Prime contractor: General Dynamics
Total number of contractors: 193

Fiscal year 2013 funding requested: $127.6 million

Program Costs (then-year dollars in millions)

	First APB (02/2008)	Latest Estimate (09/2012)
Life-cycle cost estimate	$1,969.0	$2,095.3
Acquisition	1,852.5	1,971.9
Operations and maintenance	116.5	123.4
Amount spent to date (as of September 2012)	$1,155.87	

System Deployment Details (as of December 2012)

Current number of total expected users: 17,932 of 24,483
Current number of total expected locations: 404 of 682

Legacy system to be replaced: 0
Annual cost of legacy system: not applicable

Number of system interfaces: 32

Cost, Schedule, and Performance Summary

» Exceeded planned cost estimate

» Exceeded within planned schedule estimate

» Met system performance targets

Source: Data reported by DOD officials.

TMC

Program Status

All of the products included in TMC are post development and in production. The program is currently working to sustain deployed versions of TMC hardware and software, as well as to develop new versions that are intended to add additional features, improve scalability, and enhance performance. Additionally, the program is currently fielding products to additional Army units and fielding a technical refresh to other required units.

Exceeded Planned Cost Estimate

TMC's planned total life-cycle cost estimate has increased by 6 percent from the program's first APB estimate of approximately $1.97 billion. Specifically, as of September 2012, the life-cycle cost estimate was approximately $2.1 billion. Program officials reported that the increased costs were due, in part, to the impact of several scope increases that the Army made, including the addition of new Mission Command Collapse requirements into the TMC baseline, such as the development of an architecture that provides for global scalability of Command Post of the Future's collaborative environment;[1] the implementation of previously deferred requirements; and the addition of a technology developed by the Defense Advanced Research Projects Administration, called Personalized Assistant that Learns (which enables units to automate staff procedures and tasks). The program is in the process of updating its APB, but as of January 2013, program officials were uncertain when it would be approved.

Stayed within Planned Schedule Estimate

TMC is expected to be fully deployed in September 2018, which is consistent with the program's first APB schedule estimate. In January 2009, the program received approval to fully field TMC's Command Post of the Future product to the Army, which it achieved 1 year ahead of schedule. Program officials stated that this early fielding was a result of a new approach of releasing products on a more frequent basis.

Met System Performance Targets

TMC met all three of its key performance parameters in fiscal year 2012, including supporting net-centric military operations and displaying the common operational picture. While the program did not collect objective performance metrics to gauge the system's reliability and operational effectiveness, program officials stated that use of the Command Post of the Future product in the battlefield since 2006 has served to demonstrate the operational effectiveness and reliability of the system.

---

[1]The Mission Command Collapse initiative is intended to consolidate the Army's mission command systems into a single mission command solution with an open architecture that produces a collaborative framework for the full range of warfighting functions, such as conducting intelligence operations.

Teleport Generation 3

The Defense Information System Agency's Teleport Generation 3 is intended to enable deployed forces that do not have ground-based communication systems to use various radio frequency satellite communications systems to interconnect with other forces and to access data, voice, and video communication services on the Defense Information Systems Network. Specifically, deployed forces worldwide are to be able to use various radio frequencies to connect to terminals that communicate with satellites to access the Defense Information Systems Network.

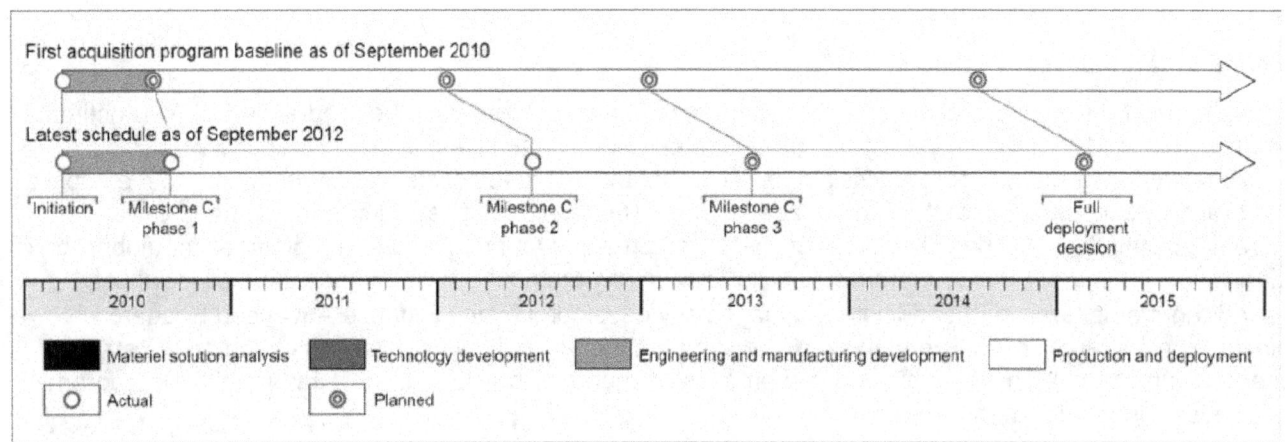

Source: GAO analysis of agency data.

Program Essentials (as of December 2012)

DOD component: Defense Information Systems Agency
Program owner: Program Executive Office - Communications

Prime contractors: (1) Space and Naval Warfare Systems Command and (2) Defense Communications and Army Transmission Systems[a]

Total number of active contractors: 9

Fiscal year 2013 funding requested: $43.1 million

Program Costs (then-year dollars in millions)

	First APB (09/2010)	Latest Estimate (09/2012)
Life-cycle cost estimate	$563.7	$581.2
Acquisition	262.5	255.6
Operations and maintenance	301.2	325.6
Amount spent to date (as of September 2012)	$113.6	

System Deployment Details (as of December 2012)

Current number of total expected users: 0 of unknown[b]
Current number of total expected locations: 0 of 9

Legacy system to be replaced: 1
Annual cost of legacy system(s): Unknown

Number of system interfaces: 5

Cost, Schedule, and Performance Summary

» Exceeded planned cost estimate

» Exceeded planned schedule estimate

» Unavailable system performance data

Source: Data reported by DOD officials.

[a] These are government entities.

[b] Defense Information Systems Agency officials indicated that the number of expected users of the Teleport system was unable to be determined. The system is intended to serve tactical users operating in every combatant command area of responsibility between 65 degrees North and 65 degrees South latitudes.

Teleport Generation 3

Program Status

Teleport Generation 3 is to be implemented in three phases. In September 2010, the program received approval to begin procuring communication terminals for phase 1 and, in July 2012, the program began installing the first of the phase 1 terminals. Additionally, in June 2012, the program began preparations for installing the first of the phase 2 terminals; however, due to delays in the testing of these terminals (discussed in more detail below), program officials were uncertain when installation of the first phase 2 terminal would begin. The program planned to request approval for procuring and installing phase 3 suites in July 2013.

Exceeded Planned Cost Estimate

Teleport Generation 3's planned total life-cycle cost estimate increased nominally by 3 percent from its first APB estimate in September 2010 of approximately $563.7 million. Specifically, the latest life-cycle cost estimate, as of September 2012, was approximately $581.2 million. Program officials attributed this increase, in part, to a more rigorous and accurate projection of operations and maintenance costs, a 3-year extension in the program's planned operations and maintenance phase, and a change in the program's schedule for purchasing and installing phase 2 terminals.

Exceeded Planned Schedule Estimate

The full deployment date for Teleport Generation 3 is not yet determined; it is expected to be set at the program's full deployment decision review, scheduled for February 2015. The program has experienced a 6-month slip in the planned date for full deployment decision compared to its first APB schedule, which was planned for August 2014. Teleport program officials attributed this slip to a delay in the testing of the phase 2 terminals, which was the responsibility of an external program office in Army's Product Manager Wideband Enterprise Satellite Systems organization. Officials reported that the testing delay affected delivery of the phase 2 terminals to Teleport sites. Additionally, the program experienced a 6-month slip in milestone C for phase 3 of the program—from January 2013 to July 2013. Program officials attributed this slip to Teleport's dependency on another DOD program that was experiencing delays and was in the process of rebaselining its schedule. Program officials plan to align Teleport's schedule with the other program's new schedule once it is approved.

Unavailable System Performance Data

As of December 2012, Teleport Generation 3 was in the early stages of implementation and, as such, had not fully implemented any terminals. Thus, system performance data were not available.

Appendix III: Comments from the Department of Defense

ASSISTANT SECRETARY OF DEFENSE
3015 DEFENSE PENTAGON
WASHINGTON, DC 20301-3015

ACQUISITION

Ms. Valerie C. Melvin
Director, Information Management
 and Technology Resources Issues
U.S. Government Accountability Office
441 G Street, N.W.
Washington, DC 20548

031213

Dear Ms. Melvin:

This is the Department of Defense (DoD) response to the GAO Draft Report, GAO-13-

311, "MAJOR AUTOMATED INFORMATION SYSTEMS: SELECTED DEFENSE

PROGRAMS NEED TO IMPLEMENT KEY ACQUISITION PRACTICES" dated February 15,

2013. Detailed comments on the report recommendations are enclosed.

Sincerely,

Ms. Katrina McFarland

Enclosure:
As stated

GAO DRAFT REPORT DATED FEBRUARY 15, 2013
GAO-13-311 (GAO CODE 310982)

"MAJOR AUTOMATED INFORMATION SYSTEMS: SELECTED DEFENSE
PROGRAMS NEED TO IMPLEMENT KEY ACQUISITION PRACTICES"

DEPARTMENT OF DEFENSE COMMENTS
TO THE GAO RECOMMENDATIONS

RECOMMENDATION 1: To better ensure that Defense Enterprise Accounting and
Management System (DEAMS) implements effective information technology (IT) acquisition
best practices, Government Accountability Office (GAO) recommends that the Secretary of
Defense direct the Secretary of the Air Force (AF) to examine the causes for the frequent
turnover in the DEAMS program manager position, and take steps to address the causes to
prevent such frequent turnover in the future.

DoD RESPONSE: Partially concur. The original program manager and his successor
maintained their role as Program Manager (PM) with the DEAMS program per their 3-year
tenure agreements. The interim PM was in place until a new PM could be assigned. The interim
PM was not intended to complete a tenured stay in the position. The needs of the Air Force
prevailed in re-assigning the fourth DEAMS PM in May 2012 prior to the end of his planned
tour. The AF supports tenure agreements for individuals in key leadership positions and intends
that the current PM will complete his 3-year tenure agreement.

RECOMMENDATION 2: To better ensure that Global Combat Support System-Army
(GCSS-Army) implements effective risk management and project monitoring and control
practices, GAO recommends that the Secretary of Defense direct the Secretary of the Army to
direct the GCSS-Army program office to establish a comprehensive risk log that maintains an
aggregation of all up-to-date risks and associated mitigation plans.

DoD RESPONSE: Concur. After consultation and multiple meetings with the GAO Team,
Army will comply with the GAO recommendations for improving the independent verification
and validation (IV&V) and risk management processes for the GCSS-Army Program.

RECOMMENDATION 3: To better ensure that GCSS-Army implements effective risk
management and project monitoring and control practices, GAO recommends that the Secretary
of Defense direct the Secretary of the Army to direct the GCSS-Army program office to specify
the roles and responsibilities of the IV&V agent to ensure that it acts as a third party that
validates and verifies the risks and mitigation plans developed by the program office and system
integrator.

DoD RESPONSE: Concur. After consultation and multiple meetings with the GAO Team,
Army will comply with the GAO recommendations for improving the IV&V and risk
management processes for the GCSS-Army Program.

2

Appendix IV: GAO Contact and Staff Acknowledgments

GAO Contact

Valerie C. Melvin at (202) 512-6304 or melvinv@gao.gov

Staff Acknowledgments

In addition to the contact name above, the following staff also made key contributions to this report: Shannin O'Neill, Assistant Director; Rebecca Eyler; James Heisel; David Hong; Javier Irizarry; Emily Kuhn; John Ockay; and Madhav Panwar.

GAO's Mission	The Government Accountability Office, the audit, evaluation, and investigative arm of Congress, exists to support Congress in meeting its constitutional responsibilities and to help improve the performance and accountability of the federal government for the American people. GAO examines the use of public funds; evaluates federal programs and policies; and provides analyses, recommendations, and other assistance to help Congress make informed oversight, policy, and funding decisions. GAO's commitment to good government is reflected in its core values of accountability, integrity, and reliability.
Obtaining Copies of GAO Reports and Testimony	The fastest and easiest way to obtain copies of GAO documents at no cost is through GAO's website (http://www.gao.gov). Each weekday afternoon, GAO posts on its website newly released reports, testimony, and correspondence. To have GAO e-mail you a list of newly posted products, go to http://www.gao.gov and select "E-mail Updates."
Order by Phone	The price of each GAO publication reflects GAO's actual cost of production and distribution and depends on the number of pages in the publication and whether the publication is printed in color or black and white. Pricing and ordering information is posted on GAO's website, http://www.gao.gov/ordering.htm. Place orders by calling (202) 512-6000, toll free (866) 801-7077, or TDD (202) 512-2537. Orders may be paid for using American Express, Discover Card, MasterCard, Visa, check, or money order. Call for additional information.
Connect with GAO	Connect with GAO on Facebook, Flickr, Twitter, and YouTube. Subscribe to our RSS Feeds or E-mail Updates. Listen to our Podcasts. Visit GAO on the web at www.gao.gov.
To Report Fraud, Waste, and Abuse in Federal Programs	Contact: Website: http://www.gao.gov/fraudnet/fraudnet.htm E-mail: fraudnet@gao.gov Automated answering system: (800) 424-5454 or (202) 512-7470
Congressional Relations	Katherine Siggerud, Managing Director, siggerudk@gao.gov, (202) 512-4400, U.S. Government Accountability Office, 441 G Street NW, Room 7125, Washington, DC 20548
Public Affairs	Chuck Young, Managing Director, youngc1@gao.gov, (202) 512-4800 U.S. Government Accountability Office, 441 G Street NW, Room 7149 Washington, DC 20548

Please Print on Recycled Paper.

www.ingramcontent.com/pod-product-compliance
Lightning Source LLC
Chambersburg PA
CBHW080321290526
45790CB00005B/2136